Using
LISREL
for Structural
Equation
Modeling

This book is dedicated to Debra MacDonald
in appreciation for her tolerance during
my frequent absences to "run one more analysis."

Using
LISREL
for Structural Equation Modeling

A Researcher's Guide

E. KEVIN KELLOWAY

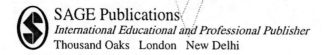

SAGE Publications
International Educational and Professional Publisher
Thousand Oaks London New Delhi

For information:

SAGE Publications, Inc.
2455 Teller Road
Thousand Oaks, California 91320
E-mail@sagepub.com

SAGE Publications Ltd.
6 Bonhill Street
London EC2A 4PU
United Kingdom

SAGE Publications India Pvt. Ltd.
M-32 Market
Greater Kailash I
New Delhi 110048 India

Printed in the United States of America

Library of Congress Cataloging-in-Publication Data

Kelloway, E. Kevin.
Using LISREL for structural equation modeling: A researcher's
guide / By E. Kevin Kelloway.
p. cm.
Includes bibliographical references and index.
ISBN 0-7619-0625-8 (acid-free paper). — ISBN 0-7619-0626-6 (pbk.:
acid-free paper)
1. LISREL. 2. Path analysis—Data processing. 3. Social
sciences—Statistical methods. I. Title. QA278.3.K45 1998
519.5'35—dc21   97-45465

98 99 00 01 02 03 04 8 7 6 5 4 3 2 1

Acquiring Editor:	Marquita Flemming
Editorial Assistant:	Frances Borghi
Production Editor:	Sanford Robinson
Editorial Assistant:	Denise Santoyo
Designer/Typesetter:	Danielle Dillahunt
Print Buyer:	Anna Chin

Contents

Acknowledgments   ix

1. Introduction   1
   Why Structural Equation Modeling?   2
   The Remainder of This Book   3

2. Structural Equation Models:
   Theory and Development   5
   The Process of Structural Equation Modeling   7
   Model Specification   7
   Identification   14
   Estimation and Fit   16
   Model Modification   20

3. Assessing Model Fit   23
   Absolute Fit   24
   Comparative Fit   29
   Parsimonious Fit   32
   Nested Model Comparisons   33
   Model Respecification   37
   Toward a Strategy for Assessing Model Fit   39

4. Using LISREL   41
   The Matrix Formulation   42
   It's All Greek to Me!   45

LISREL Keywords   *46*
Specifying the Data   *46*
Specifying the Model   *49*
Specifying the Output   *51*

5. **Confirmatory Factor Analysis**   **54**
 Model Specification   55
 From Pictures to LISREL   *56*
 Additional Comments   *61*
 Identification   62
 Estimation   63
 Assessment of Fit   77
 Model Modification   78
 Sample Results Section   78
 Results   *79*

6. **Observed Variable Path Analysis**   **81**
 Model Specification   81
 From Pictures to LISREL   *82*
 Alternative Models   *83*
 Identification   86
 Estimation   87
 Fit and Model Modification   101
 Sample Results Section   101
 Results   *101*

7. **Latent Variable Path Analysis**   **103**
 Model Specification   103
 Alternative Model Specifications   *106*
 Model Testing Strategy   *106*
 From Pictures to LISREL   *107*
 Identification and Estimation   108
 Edited Output   *111*
 Assessment and Modification   119
 From Pictures to LISREL   *120*
 Identification and Estimation II   122
 Edited Output   *123*
 Assessment and Modification II   130
 Sample Results Section   131
 Results   *131*

8. Concluding Comments   135
   Single Indicator Latent Variables   135
   Simplifying Complex Models   136
   Final Comments   137

   References   139

   Index   143

   About the Author   147

Acknowledgments

Preparation of this manuscript was supported by a Research Grant (#410-95-0155) from the Social Sciences and Humanities Research Council of Canada. I express my appreciation to Gail Hepburn, Catherine Loughlin, Morrie Mendelson, and the psychology graduate students who have taken my class in Multivariate Statistics and offered comments on earlier versions of this work.

My special appreciation goes to Julian Barling, who encouraged this and many other efforts; to Marquita Flemming of Sage, who supported the book from the beginning; and to A. J. Sobczak, who carefully edited the manuscript.

CHAPTER 1

Introduction

S ocial scientists have long been accustomed to seeing the phrase "data were analyzed with LISREL" (or a variant thereof) appear in their research literature. Indeed, some reviewers have expressed concern that LISREL analyses are dominating the literature (Brannick, 1995) at the expense of simpler forms of analyses, and some journal editors have felt compelled to point out that you do not need to use LISREL to publish in their journals (e.g., Schmitt, 1989).

Technically, of course, there is no such thing as a "LISREL" analysis. LISREL is a computer program (currently in its eighth version, Jöreskog & Sörbom, 1992) that performs structural equation modeling (SEM). The general point, however, remains. The use of structural equation modeling techniques in the social sciences is rapidly increasing (e.g., Kelloway, 1996), although there is very little evidence that such analyses are coming to dominate the literature (Kelloway, 1996; Stone-Romero, Weaver, & Glenar, 1996). One commentator has referred to the advent of SEM techniques as a statistical revolution (Cliff, 1983) and has suggested that not since the advent of analysis of variance has a statistical technique so transformed social science research. In addition to the increased usage of structural equation modeling, reviewers have pointed to the increased sophistication of such analyses (Kelloway, 1996; Medsker, Williams, & Holahan, 1994), with researchers becoming increasingly aware of the limits, constraints, and potential applications of SEM techniques.

Why Structural Equation Modeling?

Why is structural equation modeling becoming so popular? At least three reasons immediately spring to mind. First, social science research commonly uses measures to represent constructs. Most fields of social science research have a corresponding interest in measurement and measurement techniques. One form of structural equation modeling deals directly with how well our measures reflect their intended constructs. Confirmatory factor analysis, an application of structural equation modeling, is both more rigorous and more parsimonious than the "more traditional" techniques of exploratory factor analysis.

Moreover, unlike exploratory factor analysis, which is guided by intuitive and ad hoc rules, structural equation modeling casts factor analysis in the tradition of hypothesis testing, with explicit tests of both the overall quality of the factor solution and the specific parameters (e.g., factor loadings) composing the model. One of the most prevalent uses of structural equation modeling techniques is to conduct confirmatory factor analyses to assess the measurement properties of certain scales (Kelloway, 1996).

Second, aside from questions of measurement, social scientists are principally interested in questions of prediction. As our understanding of complex phenomena has grown, our predictive models have become more and more complex. Structural equation modeling techniques allow for the specification and testing of complex "path" models that incorporate this sophisticated understanding. For example, as research accumulates in an area of knowledge, our focus as researchers increasingly shifts to mediational relationships (rather than simple bivariate prediction) and the causal processes that give rise to the phenomena of interest. As I will demonstrate, the tests of these relationships available through structural equation modeling techniques are both more rigorous and more flexible than are the comparable techniques based on multiple regression.

Finally, and perhaps most important, structural equation modeling provides a unique analysis that simultaneously considers questions of both measurement and prediction. Typically referred to as "latent variable models," this form of structural equation modeling provides a flexible and powerful means of simultaneously assessing the quality of measurement and examining predictive relationships among constructs. Roughly analogous to doing a confirmatory factor analysis and path analysis at the same time, this form of structural equation modeling allows researchers to frame increasingly precise questions about the phenomena in which they are interested. Such analyses, for example, offer the considerable advantage of estimating predictive relationships among "pure" latent variables that are uncontaminated by measurement error. It is the ability to frame and test such questions to which Cliff (1983) referred when he characterized structural equation modeling as a "statistical revolution."

As even this brief discussion of structural equation modeling indicates, the primary reason for adopting such techniques is the ability to frame and answer increasingly complex questions about our data. There is considerable concern that the techniques are not readily accessible to researchers, and James and James (1989) questioned whether researchers would invest the time and energy to master a complex and still evolving form of analysis. Others have extended the concern to question whether or not the "payoff" from using structural equation modeling techniques is worth mastering a sometimes esoteric and complex literature (Brannick, 1995).

I believe that there is such a payoff. The goal of this book is to present a researcher's approach to structural equation modeling. My assumption is that the knowledge requirements of using SEM techniques consist primarily of (a) knowing the kinds of questions that SEM can help you answer, (b) knowing the kinds of assumptions you need to make (or test) about your data, and (c) knowing how the most common forms of analysis are implemented in the LISREL environment. Most important, the goal of this book is to assist you in framing and testing research questions using LISREL. Those with a taste for the more esoteric mathematical formulations are referred to the literature.

The Remainder of This Book

The remainder of this book is organized in two major sections. In the next three chapters, I present an overview of structural equation modeling, including the theory and logic of structural equation models (Chapter 2), assessing the "fit" of structural equation models to the data (Chapter 3), and the implementation of structural equation models in the LISREL environment (Chapter 4). In the second section of the book, I consider specific applications of structural equation models, including confirmatory factor analysis (Chapter 5), observed variable path analysis (Chapter 6), and latent variable path analysis (Chapter 7). For each form of model, I present a sample application including the source code, printout, and results section. Chapter 8 presents some "tricks of the trade" for structural equation modeling, including the use of single indicator latent variables and reducing the cognitive complexity of models.

Although a comprehensive understanding of structural equation modeling is a worthwhile goal, I have focused in this book on the three most common forms of analysis. In doing so, I have "glossed over" many of the refinements and types of analyses that can be performed within a structural equation modeling framework. I have also tried to stay away from features of LISREL VIII (Jöreskog & Sörbom, 1992) that are implementation-dependent. For example, I do not discuss the implementation of the SIMPLIS language or the graphical interface available in LISREL VIII. Although this choice may limit the current presentation with respect to LISREL VIII, it also makes the book relevant to users of older versions of LISREL.

When all is said and done, the intent of this book is to give a "user-friendly" introduction to structural equation modeling. The presentation is oriented to researchers who want or need to use structural equation modeling techniques to answer substantive research questions. Those interested in a more mathematical presentation are referred to the ever growing body of literature on the derivation and implementation of structural equation models.

CHAPTER 2

Structural Equation Models

Theory and Development

To begin, let us consider what we mean by the term *theory*. At one level, a theory can be thought of as an explanation of why variables are correlated (or not correlated). Of course, most theories in the social sciences go far beyond the description of correlations to include hypotheses about causal relations. A necessary but insufficient condition for the validity of a theory would be that the relationships (i.e., correlations/covariances) among variables are consistent with the propositions of the theory.

For example, consider Fishbein and Ajzen's (1975) well-known theory of reasoned action. In the theory (see Figure 2.1), the best predictor of behavior is posited as being the intention to perform the behavior. In turn, the intention to perform the behavior is thought to be caused by (a) the individual's attitude toward performing the behavior and (b) the individual's subjective norms about the behavior. Finally, attitudes toward the behavior are thought to be a function of the individual's beliefs about the behavior. This simple presentation of the theory is sufficient to generate some expectations about the pattern of correlations between the variables referenced in the theory.

If the theory is correct, then one would expect that the correlation between behavioral intentions and behavior and the correlation between beliefs and attitudes should be stronger than the correlations between

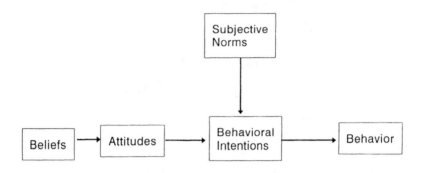

attitudes and behavior or subjective norms and behavior. Correspondingly, the correlations between beliefs and behavioral intentions and beliefs and behavior should be the weakest correlations. With reference to Figure 2.1, the general principle is that if the theory is correct, then direct and proximal relationships should be stronger than more distal relationships.

As a simple test of the theory, one could collect data on behavior, behavioral intentions, attitudes, subjective norms, and beliefs. If the theory is correct, one would expect to see the pattern of correlations described above. If the actual correlations do not conform to the pattern, one could reasonably conclude that the theory was incorrect (i.e., the model of reasoned action did not account for the observed correlations).

Note that the converse is not true. Finding the expected pattern of correlations would not imply that the theory is right, only that it is plausible. There might be other theories that would result in the same pattern of correlations (e.g., one could hypothesize that behavior causes behavioral intentions, which in turn cause attitudes and subjective norms). As noted earlier, finding the expected pattern of correlations is a necessary but not sufficient condition for the validity of the theory.

Although the above example was a simple one, it illustrates the logic of structural equation modeling. In essence, structural equation modeling is based on the observations that (a) every theory implies a set of correlations and (b) if the theory is valid, then the theory should be able to explain or reproduce the patterns of correlations found in the empirical data.

The Process of Structural Equation Modeling

The remainder of this chapter is organized according to a linear "model" of structural equation modeling. Although linear models of the research process are notoriously suspect (McGrath, Martin, & Kukla, 1982) and may not reflect actual practice, the heuristic has the advantage of drawing attention to the major concerns, issues, and decisions involved in developing and evaluating structural equation modeling. Bollen and Long (1993, pp. 1-2) describe the five stages characteristic of most applications of structural equation modeling:

1. model specification,
2. identification,
3. estimation,
4. testing fit, and
5. respecification.

For presentation purposes, I will defer much of the discussion of testing fit until the next chapter.

Model Specification

Structural equation modeling is inherently a confirmatory technique. That is, for reasons that will become clear as the discussion progresses, the methods of structural equation modeling are ill suited for the exploratory identification of relationships. Rather, the foremost requirement for any form of structural equation modeling is the a priori specification of a model. The propositions composing the model are most frequently drawn from previous research or theory (Bollen & Long, 1993), although the role of informed judgment, hunches, and dogmatic statements of belief should not be discounted. However derived, the purpose of the model is to explain why variables are correlated in a particular fashion. Bollen (1989, p. 1), for example, presents the fundamental hypothesis for structural equation modeling as:

$$\Sigma = \Sigma(\Theta)$$

where Σ is the observed population covariance matrix, Θ is a vector of model parameters, and $\Sigma(\Theta)$ is the covariance matrix implied by the model. When the equality expressed in the equation holds, the model is said to "fit" the data. Thus, the goal of structural equation modeling is to explain the patterns of covariance observed among the study variables.

In essence, then, a model is an explanation of why two (or more) variables are related (or not). In undergraduate statistics courses, we often harp on the observation that a correlation between X and Y has at least three possible interpretations (i.e., X causes Y, Y causes X, or X and Y are both caused by a third variable Z). In formulating a model, you are choosing one of these explanations, in full recognition of the fact that either of the remaining two might be just as good, or better, explanations.

It follows from these observations that the "model" used to explain the data cannot be derived from that data. For any covariance or correlation matrix, one can always derive a model that provides a perfect fit to the data. Rather, the power of structural equation modeling derives from the attempt to assess the fit of theoretically derived predictions to the data.

It might help at this point to consider two types of variables. In any study, we have variables we want to explain or predict. We also have variables that we think will offer the explanation or prediction we desire. The former are known as *endogenous* variables, whereas the latter are *exogenous* variables. Exogenous variables are considered to be the starting points of the model. We are not interested in how the exogenous variables came about. Endogenous variables may serve as both predictors and criteria, being predicted by exogenous variables and predicting other endogenous variables. A model, then, is a set of theoretical propositions that link the exogenous variables to the endogenous variables and the endogenous variables to one another. Taken as a whole, the model explains both what relationships we expect to see in the data and what relationships we do not expect to emerge.

It is worth repeating that the fit of a model to data, in itself, conveys no information about the validity of the underlying theory. Thankfully, the misnomer (Breckler, 1990) "causal modeling" appears to have passed out of fashion, with the recognition that structural equation models do not assess or "prove" causality any more than the application of any statistical technique conveys information about the causal relations in the data (Williams, 1995).

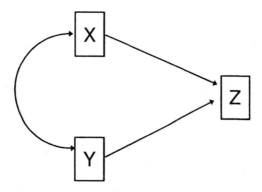

Figure 2.2.

Although the hypotheses underlying model development may be causal in nature, assessing the fit of a model does not provide a basis for causal inference (Brannick, 1995; Kelloway, 1995; Williams, 1995). The conditions necessary for causal inference in structural equation modeling are presented by James and colleagues (James, Mulaik, & Brett, 1982) and are more briefly summarized by Bollen (1989) as three main conditions: (a) association, (b) isolation (the inclusion of all relevant predictors), and (c) the establishment of causal direction. Meeting these conditions for causal inference is more a matter of study design than of statistical technique.

Path diagrams. Most frequently, the structural relations that form the model are depicted in a path diagram in which variables are linked by unidirectional arrows (representing causal relations) or bidirectional curved arrows (representing noncausal, or correlational, relationships).[1] Consider three variables X, Y, and Z. A possible path diagram depicting the relationships among the three is given in Figure 2.2.

The diagram presents two exogenous variables (X and Y) that are assumed to be correlated (curved arrow). Both variables are presumed to cause Z (unidirectional arrows).

Now consider adding a fourth variable, Q, with the hypotheses that Q is caused by both X and Z, with no direct effect of Y on Q. The path diagram representing these hypotheses is presented in Figure 2.3.

Three important assumptions underlie path diagrams. First, it is assumed that all of the proposed causal relations are linear. Although

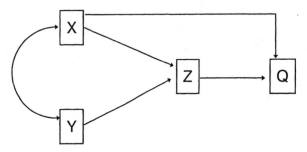

Figure 2.3.

there are ways of approximating nonlinear relations in structural equation modeling (see Kenny & Judd, 1984), for the most part we are concerned only with linear relations. Second, path diagrams are assumed to represent all the causal relations between the variables. It is just as important to specify the causal relationships that do exist as it is to specify the relationships that do not. Finally, path diagrams are based on the assumption of causal closure; this is the assumption that all causes of the variables in the model are represented in the model. That is, any variable thought to cause two or more variables in the model should in itself be part of the model. Failure to actualize this assumption results in misleading and often inflated results (which economists refer to as specification error). In general, we are striving for the most parsimonious diagram that (a) fully explains why variables are correlated and (b) can be justified on theoretical grounds.

Finally, it should be noted that one can also think of factor analysis as a path diagram. The common factor model on which all factor analyses are based states that the responses to an individual item are a function of (a) the trait that the item is measuring and (b) error. Another way to phrase this is that the observed variables (items) are a function of both common factors and unique factors.

For example, consider the case of six items that are thought to load on two factors (which are oblique). Diagrammatically, we can represent this model as shown in Figure 2.4. Note that this is the conceptual model that we have when planning a factor analysis. As will be explained in greater detail later, the model represents the confirmatory factor analysis model and not the model commonly used for exploratory factor analysis.

In the diagram, F1 and F2 are the two common factors. They are also referred to as *latent variables* or unobserved variables because they are

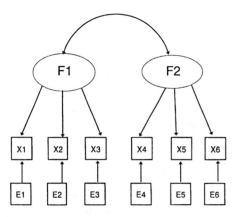

Figure 2.4.

not measured directly. Note that it is common to represent latent variables in ovals or circles. X1 . . . X6 are the *observed* or *manifest variables* (test items, sometimes called indicators), whereas E1 . . . E6 are the residuals (sometimes called unique factors or error variances). Thus, although most of this presentation focuses on path diagrams, all the material is equally relevant to factor analysis, which can be thought of as a special form of path analysis.

Converting the path diagram to structural equations. Path diagrams are most useful in depicting the hypothesized relations because there is a set of rules that allow one to translate the diagram into a series of structural equations. The rules, initially developed by Sewall Wright (1934), allow one to write a set of equations that completely define the observed correlations matrix.

The logic and rules for path analysis are quite straightforward. The set of arrows constituting the path diagram include both simple and compound paths. A *simple path* (e.g., $X \rightarrow Y$) represents the direct relationship between two variables (i.e., the regression of Y on X). A compound path (e.g., $X \rightarrow Y \rightarrow Z$) consists of two or more simple paths. The value of a compound path is the product of all the simple paths constituting the compound path. Finally, and most important for our purposes, the correlation between any two variables is the sum of the simple and compound paths linking the two variables.

Given this background, Sewall Wright's rules for decomposing correlations are these:

1. After going forward on an arrow, the path cannot go backward. The path can, however, go backward as many times as necessary prior to going forward.
2. The path cannot go through the same construct more than once.
3. The path can include only one curved arrow.

Consider, for example, three variables, A, B, and C. Following psychological precedent, I measure these variables in a sample of 100 undergraduates and produce the following correlation matrix:

	A	B	C
A	1.00		
B	.50	1.00	
C	.65	.70	1.00

I believe that both A and B are causal influences on C. Diagrammatically, my model might look like the model shown in Figure 2.5.

Following the standard rules for computing path coefficients, I can write a series of structural equations to represent these relationships. By solving for the variables in the structural equations, I am computing the path coefficients (the values of the simple paths).

$$c = .5$$

$$a + cb = .65 \tag{2.1}$$

$$b + ca = .70 \tag{2.2}$$

Note that three equations completely define the correlation matrix. That is, each correlation is thought to result from the relationships specified in the model. Those who still recall high school algebra will recognize that I have three equations to solve for three unknowns; therefore, the solution is straightforward. Because I know the value of c (from the correlation matrix), I begin by substituting c into Equations 2.1 and 2.2. Equation 2.1 then becomes

$$a + .5b = .65 \tag{2.1.1}$$

and Equation 2.2 becomes

$$b + .5a = .70 \tag{2.2.1}$$

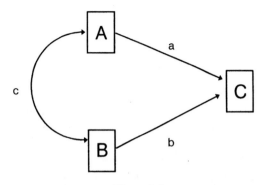

Figure 2.5.

To solve the equations, one can multiply Equation 2.2.1 by 2 (resulting in Equation 2.2.2) and then subtract Equation 2.1.1 from the result.

$$2b + a = 1.4 \qquad (2.2.2)$$

$$- (.5b + a = .65 \qquad (2.1.1)$$

$$= 1.5b \qquad = .75 \qquad (2.3)$$

From Equation 2.3, we can solve for b: $b = .75/1.5 = .50$. Substituting b into either Equation 2.2.1 or Equation 2.1.1 results in $a = .40$. Thus, the three path values are $a = .40$, $b = .50$, and $c = .50$.

These numbers are standardized partial regression coefficients or beta weights and are interpreted exactly the same as betas derived from multiple regression analyses. Indeed, a simpler method to derive the path coefficients a and b would have been to use a statistical package to conduct an ordinary least squares regression of C on A and B. The important point is that any model implies a set of structural relations among the variables. These structural relations can be represented as a set of structural equations and, in turn, imply a correlation (or covariance) matrix.

Thus, a simple check on the accuracy of the solution is to work backwards. Using the estimates of structural parameters, we can calculate the correlation matrix. If the matrix is the same as the one we started out with, we have reached the correct solution. Thus,

$$c = .5$$
$$a + cb = .65$$
$$b + ca = .70$$

and we have calculated that $b = .5$ and $a = .4$. Substituting into the second equation above, we get $.4 + .5 \times .5 = .65$ or $.4 + .25 = .65$. For the second equation, we get $.5 + .5 \times .4 = .70$, or $.5 + .20 = .70$. In this case, our model was able to reproduce the correlation matrix. That is, we were able to find a set of regression or path weights for the model that can replicate the original, observed, correlations.

Identification

As illustrated by the foregoing example, application of structural equation modeling techniques involves the estimation of unknown parameters (e.g., factor loadings or path coefficients) based on observed covariances/correlations. In general, issues of identification deal with whether a unique solution for the model (or its component parameters) can be obtained (Bollen, 1989). Models and/or parameters may be underidentified, just-identified, or overidentified (Pedhazur, 1982).

In the example given above, the number of structural equations composing the model exactly equals the number of unknowns (i.e., three unknowns and three equations). In such a case, the model is said to be *just-identified* (because there is just one correct answer). A just-identified model will always provide a unique solution (i.e., set of path values) that will be able to perfectly reproduce the correlation matrix. A just-identified model is also referred to as a saturated model (Medsker et al., 1994).

A necessary, but insufficient, condition for the identification of a structural equation model is that one cannot estimate more parameters than there are unique elements in the covariance matrix. Bollen (1989) refers to this as the "t rule" for model identification. Given a $k \times k$ covariance matrix (where k is the number of variables), there are $k \times (k - 1)/2$ unique elements in the covariance matrix. Attempts to estimate exactly $k \times (k - 1)/2$ parameters results in the just-identified or "saturated" (Medsker et al., 1994) model. Only one unique solution is obtainable for the just-identified model, and the model always provides a perfect fit to the data.

When the number of unknowns exceeds the number of equations, the model is said to be *underidentified*. This is a problem because the model parameters cannot uniquely ascertained; there is no unique solution. Consider, for example, the solution to the equation $X + Y = 10$. There are no two unique values for X and Y that solve this equation (there are, however, an infinite number of possibilities).

Last, and most important, when the number of equations exceeds the number of unknowns, the model is *overidentified*. When models are overidentified, there are a number of unique solutions, and the task in most applications of structural equation modeling techniques is to find the solution that provides the best fit to the data. Thus, the identification of a structural equation model is purely a matter of the number of estimated parameters (Bollen, 1989).

The ideal situation for the social scientist is to have an overidentified model. If the model is underidentified, no solution is possible. If the model is just-identified, then there is one set of values that completely fit the observed correlation matrix. That matrix, however, also contains many sources of error (e.g., sampling error, measurement error). In an overidentified model, there are a number of possible solutions, and the task is to select the one that comes closest to explaining the observed data within some margin of error. We always, therefore, want our models to be overidentified.

Although it is always possible to "prove" that your proposed model is overidentified (see Long, 1983a, 1983b for examples), the procedures are cumbersome and involve extensive calculations. Overidentification of a structural equation model is achieved by placing two types of restrictions on the model parameters to be estimated.

First, researchers assign a direction to parameters. In effect, positing a model based on one-way causal flow restricts half of the posited parameters to be zero. Models incorporating such a one-way causal flow are known as *recursive models*. Bollen (1989) points out that recursiveness is a sufficient condition for model identification. That is, as long as all the arrows are going in the same direction, the model is identified. Moreover, in the original formulation of path analysis, where path coefficients are estimated through OLS regression (Pedhazur, 1982), recursiveness is a required property of models. Recursive models, however, are not a necessary condition for identification, and it is possible to estimate identified nonrecursive models (i.e., models that incorporate reciprocal causation) using programs such as LISREL.

Second, researchers achieve overidentification by setting some parameters to be fixed to a predetermined value. Typically, values of specific parameters are set to zero. Earlier, in the discussion of model specification, I made the point that it is important for researchers to consider (a) what paths will be in the model and (b) which paths are not in the model. By "not in the model," I am referring to the setting of certain paths to zero. For example, in the theory of reasoned action presented earlier (see Figure 2.1), several potential paths (i.e., from attitudes to behavior, from norms to behavior, from beliefs to intentions, from beliefs to norms, and from beliefs to behavior) were set to zero to achieve overidentification. Had these paths been included in the model, the model would be just-identified.

Estimation and Fit

If the model is overidentified, then, by definition, there are an infinite number of solutions. Moreover, given moderately complex models, solving the structural equations by hand would quickly become a formidable problem. Indeed, the growing popularity of structural equation modeling is probably most attributable to the availability of software packages such as LISREL that are designed to solve sets of structural equations.

LISREL solves these equations (as do most similar programs) by using numerical methods to estimate parameters. In particular, LISREL solves for model parameters by a process of iterative estimation. To illustrate the process of iterative estimation, consider a common children's guessing game.

When I was a boy, we played a game called hot, hotter, hottest. In one version of the game, one child would pick a number and the other child would attempt to guess the number. If the guess was close, the guesser was "getting hotter." If the guess was way off, the guesser was "getting colder." By a simple process of informed trial and error, you could almost always guess the number.

This is precisely the process LISREL uses to estimate model parameters. The program starts by taking a "guess" at the parameter values. It then calculates the implied covariance matrix (the covariance matrix that would result from that set of model parameters). The implied covariance matrix is then compared to the observed covariance matrix (i.e., the actual data) to see how "hot" the first guess was. If the guess was right (i.e., if the implied and actual covariance matrices are very similar), the process stops. If the guess was wrong, then LISREL adjusts the first guess (the starting values) and checks again. This process of iterative estimation continues until some fitting criterion has been achieved (the solution is "red hot").

How does LISREL know when it is "red hot"—that is, when the correct answer is obtained? In general, the user specifies a fitting criterion (a mathematical function) that the program tries to minimize. When repeated iterations fail to minimize the fitting criterion, LISREL grinds to a halt and reports the last solution it estimated. Three very common fitting criteria are ordinary least squares (OLS), generalized least squares (GLS), and maximum likelihood (ML). In matrix notation, these criteria are defined as

$$OLS = tr(S - C)^2$$

$$GLS = 1/2 \; tr[(S - C)S^{-1}]^2$$

$$ML = \ln|C| - \ln|S| + tr \; SC^{-1} - m$$

where   tr = trace (sum of the diagonal elements),

   S = covariance matrix implied by the model,

   C = actual covariance matrix,

   ln = natural logarithm, and

   | | indicates the determinant (index of generalized variance) of a matrix.

Although the specifics of the equations are not important, it is important to note that each criterion attempts to minimize the differences between the implied and observed covariance matrices. That is, each equation has as its basis the direct comparison of S and C. When the observed and predicted covariance matrices are exactly the same, all the above criteria will equal 0. Conversely, when the matrices are different, the value of the fitting function gets larger. Thus, the goal of the iterative estimation procedure used by LISREL is to minimize the fitting function specified by the user.

Because of the complexity of the subject, we will defer further discussion of assessing model fit until the next chapter. Three additional issues regarding model estimation should be noted, however: the choice of estimators, the choice of data type, and sample size requirements.

Choice of Estimators

Perhaps the most widely used type of estimation is maximum likelihood, followed by generalized least squares (Anderson & Gerbing, 1988; Kelloway, 1996). Maximum likelihood estimation is so popular that researchers seem to equate using LISREL with doing maximum likelihood estimation (Kelloway, 1996), even though LISREL allows a variety of estimation techniques.

Maximum likelihood estimators are known to be consistent and asymptotically efficient in large samples (Bollen, 1989). The popularity of these methods, however, is more likely attributable to the fact that (under certain conditions) the minimum of the fitting criterion multiplied by $N - 1$ (where N is the number of observations) is distributed as χ^2. For maximum likelihood estimation, if we have a large sample and are willing to assume (or show) that the observed variables are multivariate normal, then the χ^2 test is reasonable. If we have a large sample but are not willing to assume multivariate normality, then GLS estimation is the method of choice.

Although most readers will be familiar with Ordinary Least Squares estimation as used in multiple regression, maximum likelihood and generalized least squares estimation are slightly different. Ordinary least squares is known as a partial information technique, whereas both maximum likelihood estimation and generalized least squares are full information techniques. To understand this distinction, consider the diagram of the Fishbein and Ajzen (1975) theory of reasoned action presented in Figure 2.1.

As mentioned earlier, one way to solve for the path values in this model would be to conduct a series of three regression analyses. That is, one would regress the following:

1. behavior on behavioral intentions,
2. behavioral intentions on subjective norms and attitudes, and
3. attitudes on beliefs.

If you were to follow this strategy, then each path value would be estimated independently of the others. If, for example, you made a mistake in calculating the value for the path relating beliefs to attitudes, that would not affect the value of the path leading from behavioral intentions to behavior.

In contrast, maximum likelihood estimation is a full information technique. Simply put, in using maximum likelihood estimation, one estimates all the parameters (i.e., path values) simultaneously. In this case, an error in one value (e.g., a poorly specified part of the model) will be reflected in every parameter estimated.

The consequences of using full information techniques as opposed to partial information techniques are potentially serious (Brannick, 1995) but as yet poorly understood (Williams, 1995). In particular, the advantages of full information techniques (i.e., the availability of hypothesis testing) may outweigh the potential disadvantages. Moreover, under many circumstances, maximum likelihood estimation and ordinary least squares will result in identical estimates, lending weight to the use of full information techniques.

Choice of Data

Up until this point, I have been using the terms *correlation matrix* and *covariance matrix* interchangeably. The two matrices are very similar. A covariance matrix has measures of covariance in the off-diagonal positions, with measures of variance in the main diagonal. A correlation matrix is simply a standardized covariance matrix (i.e., because all the variables are standardized, a correlation matrix has 1s in the main diagonal).

Although the matrices are very similar, the standardization of variables in constructing a correlation matrix removes important information about the scale of measurement of individual variables from the data. This is an important concern because many types of structural equation models are not scale invariant (Cudeck, 1989). That is, one will get different results depending on whether the analysis is based on a correlation or a covariance matrix.

Some authors have suggested that the choice of a correlation or a covariance matrix for input is based on both theoretical concerns and the preferences of some disciplines. Theoretically, if one is concerned only with the pattern of relationships among variables, a correlation matrix is an appropriate choice. Indeed, use of a correlation matrix simplifies interpretation of the results by rescaling all variables to have unit variance. Moreover, use of the correlation matrix may result in more conservative estimates of parameter significance (generally held to be desirable in statistics).

Having said this, use of the covariance matrix is strongly recommended in virtually all instances. Structural equation models are not always scale free—thus, a model that fits the correlation matrix may not fit the covariance matrix. Moreover, the hypothesis tests available in structural equation modeling are based on the assumption that one is analyzing a covariance matrix. Thus, although there may be valid reasons to analyze a correlation matrix, use of the covariance matrix generally is recommended. This general recommendation applies with equal force to all the types of analysis discussed here.

Sample Size

Although it may not have been obvious up until this point, structural equation modeling is very much a large sample technique. Both the estimation methods (e.g., maximum likelihood) and tests of model fit (e.g., the χ^2 test) are based on the assumption of large samples. Several authors have presented guidelines on the definition of "large" (e.g., Anderson & Gerbing, 1984; Bentler & Chou, 1987; Marsh, Balla, & MacDonald, 1988).

In general, it seems that a sample size of at least 200 observations would be an appropriate minimum. For example, it is commonly recommended that models incorporating latent variables require at least a sample size of 100 observations, although parameter estimates may be inaccurate in samples of less than 200 (Marsh et al., 1988). Boomsma (1983) recommends a sample size of approximately 200 for models of moderate complexity. Taking a somewhat different approach, Bentler and Chou (1987) have suggested that the ratio of sample size to estimated parameters be between 5:1 and 10:1 (similar to frequently cited guidelines for regression analyses, e.g., Tabachnick & Fidell, 1996).

Model Modification

Perhaps no aspect of structural equation modeling techniques is more controversial than the role of model respecification. The goal of model respecification is to improve either the parsimony or the fit of the model (MacCallum, 1986). Thus, respecification typically consists of one of two forms of model modification. First, researchers may delete nonsignificant paths from their models in a "theory-trimming" (Pedhazur, 1982) approach. Second, researchers may add paths to the model based on the empirical results.

Although model respecification frequently is included in descriptions of the modeling process (e.g., Bollen & Long, 1993), there are several problems with specification searches. Perhaps most important, the available data suggest that specification searches typically do not retrieve the actual model (MacCallum, 1986). Moreover, because specification

searches are conducted post hoc and are empirically rather than theoretically derived, model modifications based on such searches must be
validated on an independent sample. As James and James (1989) point
out, it is perfectly acceptable to modify the model and assess the fit of
the model based on data from one sample; it is the interpretation of such
model modifications that is suspect. When models are modified and
reassessed on the same data, parameters added to or deleted from the
model cannot be said to be confirmed.

Aside from the exploratory nature of model respecifications, there is
considerable doubt about the meaning of parameters added to a model
based on a specification search. Certainly, there are examples in the
literature (and in my own work; see Barling, Kelloway, & Bremmerman,
1991) of adding substantively uninterpretable parameters (e.g., covariances among error terms) to a model to improve the fit of the model.
Such parameters have been termed "wastebasket" parameters (Browne,
1982), and there is little justification for their inclusion in structural
models (Kelloway, 1995, 1996).

It is tempting to conclude, as I have previously (Kelloway, 1996), that
parameters that can be assigned a substantive meaning are "legitimate"
additions to a structural model during a specification search. Steiger
(1990, p. 175) pointed to the flaw in this conclusion when he questioned, " What percentage of researchers would find themselves unable
to think up a 'theoretical justification' for freeing a parameter? In the
absence of empirical information to the contrary, I assume that the
answer . . . is 'near zero.' "

Although replication of model modifications on an independent
sample is commonly recognized to be an appropriate strategy, it should
be noted that there are also problems with this strategy. Perhaps most
important, because the empirically driven respecification of model
parameters capitalizes on chance variations in the data, the results of
such replication efforts may be inconsistent (MacCallum, Roznowski,
& Necowitz, 1992). Thus, there are both conceptual and empirical
problems with the practice of respecifying models and, at best, such
respecifications provide limited information.

So what do you do if your model doesn't fit the data? One solution
to an ill-fitting model is to simply stop testing and declare the theory
that guided model development to be wrong. This approach has the
advantage of conforming to a classical decision-making view of hypothesis testing; that is, you have a hypothesis, you perform a test, and you
either accept or reject the hypothesis. The disadvantage of this approach
is, of course, that one does not gain any insight into what the "correct"

(or at least one plausible) theory might be. In particular, there is information in the data you have collected that you may not be using to its fullest advantage.

A second approach to an ill-fitting model is to use the available information to try to generate a more appropriate model. This is the "art" of model modification—changing the original model to fit the data. Although model modification is fraught with perils, I do not believe that anyone has ever "gotten it right" on the first attempt at model fitting. Thus, the art of model fitting is to understand the dangers and try to account for them when you alter your model based on empirical observations.

The principal danger in post hoc model modification is that this procedure is exploratory and involves considerable capitalization on chance. Thus, you might add a path to a model to make it fit the data only to find that you have capitalized on chance variation within your sample and the results will never be replicated in another sample. There are at least two strategies for minimizing this problem.

First, try to make model modifications that have some semblance of theoretical consistency (bearing in mind Steiger's comments about our ability to rationalize). If there are 20 studies suggesting that job satisfaction and job performance are unrelated, do not hypothesize a path between satisfaction and performance just to make your model fit. Second, as with any scientific endeavor, models are worthwhile only when they can be replicated in another sample. Post hoc modifications to a model should always be (a) identified as such and (b) replicated in another sample.[2]

Notes

1. It also helps to remember that in path diagrams, the hypothesized causal "flow" is traditionally from left to right (or top to bottom); that is, the independent (exogenous) variables or predictors are on the left (top), and the dependent (endogenous) variables or criteria are on the right (bottom).

2. Note that the use of a holdout sample is often recommended for this purpose. Set aside 25% of the original sample, then test and modify the model on the remaining 75%. When you have a model that fits the data on the original 75%, test the model on the remaining 25%. Although this procedure does not always result in replicated findings, it can help identify which paths are robust and which are not.

CHAPTER 3

Assessing Model Fit

Perhaps more has been written about the assessment of model fit than any other aspect of structural equation modeling. Indeed, many researchers are attracted to structural equation modeling techniques because of the availability of global measures of model fit (Brannick, 1995). In practice, such measures often are used as an omnibus test of the model whereby one first assesses global fit before proceeding to a consideration of the individual parameters composing the model (Jöreskog, 1993). A variety of fit indices are currently available to researchers wishing to assess the fit of their models, and it is instructive to consider exactly what we mean when we claim that a model "fits" the data.

At least two traditions in the assessment of model fit are apparent (Tanaka, 1993): the assessment of the *absolute* fit of the model and the assessment of the *comparative* fit of the model. The assessment of the comparative fit of the model may be further subdivided into the assessment of comparative fit and *parsimonious* fit. The assessment of absolute fit is concerned with the ability of the model to reproduce the actual covariance matrix. The assessment of comparative fit is concerned with comparing two or more competing models to assess which provides the better fit to the data.

The assessment of parsimonious fit is based on the recognition that one can always obtain a better fitting model by estimating more parameters. (At the extreme, one can always obtain a perfect fit to the data by estimating the just-identified model containing all possible parameters.) Thus, the assessment of parsimonious fit is based on the idea of a "cost-benefit" trade-off and asks: Is the cost (loss of a degree of freedom) worth the additional benefit (increased fit) of estimating more parameters? Although measures of comparative and absolute fit will always favor more complex models, measures of parsimonious fit provide a "fairer" basis for comparison by adjusting for the known effects of estimating more parameters.

In the remainder of this chapter, I present the most commonly used indices for assessing absolute, comparative, and parsimonious fit. Of necessity, the presentation is based on the formulae for calculating these indices; however, it should be remembered that structural equation modeling programs such as LISREL do the actual calculations for you. The researcher's task, therefore, is to understand what the fit indices are measuring and how they should be interpreted. The chapter concludes with some recommendations on assessing the fit of models.

Absolute Fit

Tests of absolute fit are concerned with the ability to reproduce the correlation/covariance matrix. As shown in the previous chapter, perhaps the most straightforward test of this ability is to work backwards, that is, from the derived parameter estimates, calculate the implied covariance matrix and compare it, item by item, with the observed matrix. There are at least two major stumbling blocks to this procedure.

First, the computations are laborious when models are even moderately complex. Second, there are no hard and fast standards of how "close" the implied and observed covariance matrices must be to claim that the model fits the data. For example, if the actual correlation between two variables is 0.45 and the correlation implied by the model is 0.43, does the model fit the data or not?

Early in the history of structural equation modeling, researchers recognized that for some methods of estimation a single test statistic (distributed as χ^2) was available to test the null hypothesis that

$$\Sigma = \Sigma(\Theta)$$

where Σ is the population covariance matrix and $\Sigma(\Theta)$ is the covariance matrix implied by the model (Bollen & Long, 1993). The development of the χ^2 test statistic for structural equation models proceeds directly from early accounts of path analysis in which the attempt was to specify

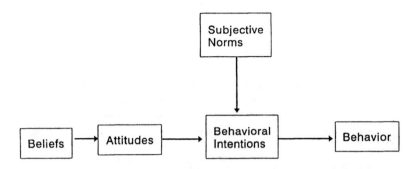

Figure 3.1.

a model that reproduced the original covariance matrix (e.g., Blalock, 1964). In the obverse of traditional hypothesis testing, a nonsignificant χ^2 implies that there is no significant discrepancy between the covariance matrix implied by the model and the population covariance matrix. Hence, a nonsignificant χ^2 indicates that the model "fits" the data in that the model can reproduce the population covariance matrix.

The test is distributed with degrees of freedom equal to

$$1/2(q)(q + 1) - k$$

where q = the number of variables in the model and

k = the number of estimated parameters.

For example, the Fishbein and Ajzen (1975) model introduced in Chapter 2 and repeated in Figure 3.1 is based on five variables and incorporates four paths:

1. Behavioral intentions predict behavior.
2. Attitudes predict behavioral intentions.
3. Subjective norms predict behavioral intentions.
4. Beliefs predict attitudes.

The model therefore has

$$df = 1/2(5)(6) - 4$$
$$df = 1/2(30) - 4$$

$$df = 15 - 4$$
$$df = 11.$$

Although the test is quite simple (indeed, LISREL calculates it for you), there are some problems with the χ^2 test in addition to the logical problem of being required to accept the null hypothesis. First, the approximation to the χ^2 distribution occurs only for large samples (e.g., $N \geq 200$). Second, just at the point where the χ^2 distribution becomes a tenable assumption, the test has a great deal of power. Recall that the test is calculated as $N - 1 \times$ (the minimum of the fitting function); therefore, as N increases, the value of χ^2 must also increase. Thus, for a minimum fitting function of .5, the resulting χ^2 value would be 99.5 for $N = 200$, 149.5 for $N = 300$, and so on. This makes it highly unlikely that you will be able to obtain a nonsignificant test statistic with large sample sizes.

Although not typically presented as fit indices, the LISREL output also includes some indications of model fit, including the following:

1. the noncentrality parameter (estimated as $\chi^2 - df$ and used in the calculation of some fit indices),
2. the 90% confidence interval for the noncentrality parameter,
3. the minimum of the fitting function,
4. the discrepancy function (used in calculating other fit indices), and
5. the 90% confidence interval for the discrepancy function.

This output is presented largely for the information of the researcher, and the values presented typically have no straightforward interpretation. As noted above, however, much of this information is used in the calculation of other fit indices, as explained below.

Given the known problems of the χ^2 test as an assessment of model fit, numerous alternate fit indices have been proposed. Gerbing and Anderson (1992, p. 134) describe the ideal properties of such indices to

1. indicate degree of fit along a continuum bounded by values such as 0 and 1, where 0 represents a lack of fit and 1 reflects perfect fit.
2. be independent of sample size. . . . and
3. have known distributional characteristics to assist interpretation and allow the construction of a confidence interval.

With the possible exception of the root mean squared error of approximation (Steiger, 1990; see below), thus far none of the fit indices commonly reported in the literature satisfy all three of these criteria; the requirement for known distributional characteristics is particularly lacking. The current version of LISREL (LISREL VIII) reports 18 such indices of model fit, only four of which address the question of absolute fit.

The simplest fit index provided by LISREL is root mean squared residual (RMR). This is the square root of the mean of the squared discrepancies between the implied and observed covariance matrices. The lower bound of the index is 0, and low values are taken to indicate good fit. The index, however, is sensitive to the scale of measurement of the model variables. As a result, it is difficult to determine what a "low" value actually is. LISREL therefore also now provides the standardized RMR, which has a lower bound of 0 and an upper bound of 1. Generally for this index, values less than 0.05 are interpreted as indicating a good fit to the data.

LISREL also reports the root mean squared error of approximation (RMSEA) developed by Steiger (1990). Similar to the RMR, the RMSEA is based on the analysis of residuals, with smaller values indicating a better fit to the data. Steiger (1990) suggests that values below 0.10 indicate a good fit to the data, and values below 0.05 a very good fit to the data. Values below 0.01 indicate an outstanding fit to the data, although Steiger (1990) notes that these values rarely are obtained.

Unlike all other fit indices discussed in this chapter, the RMSEA has the important advantage of going beyond point estimates to the provision of 90% confidence intervals for the point estimate. Moreover, LISREL also provides a test of the significance of the RMSEA by testing whether the value obtained is significantly different from 0.05 (the value that Steiger suggests indicates a very good fit to the data). Perhaps because of its recent inclusion in the LISREL program, the RMSEA is not frequently reported in the literature; however, the advantages of confidence intervals and formal hypothesis testing available with this index will likely increase its use as a measure of model fit.

The goodness-of-fit index (GFI) is based on a ratio of the sum of the squared discrepancies to the observed variances (for generalized least squares, the maximum likelihood version is somewhat more complicated). The GFI ranges from 0 to 1, with values exceeding 0.9 indicating a good fit to the data. It should be noted that this guideline is based on experience. Like many of the fit indices that will be presented, the GFI has no known sampling distribution. As a result, "rules" about when an index indicates a good fit to the data are highly arbitrary and should be treated with caution.

Finally, the adjusted goodness-of-fit index (AGFI) adjusts the GFI for degrees of freedom in the model. The AGFI also ranges from 0 to 1, with values above 0.9 indicating a good fit to the data. A discrepancy between the GFI and AGFI typically indicates the inclusion of trivial (i.e., small) and often nonsignificant parameters.

Early in the discussion of fit indices, researchers proposed assessing the fit of the model by taking the ratio of the χ^2 and its degrees of freedom. Unfortunately, conflicting standards of interpretation for this index abound (Medsker et al., 1994). For example, χ^2/df ratios of less than 5 have been interpreted as indicating a good fit to the data as have ratios between 2 and 5, with ratios less than 2 indicating overfitting. Interpretative standards for the χ^2/df ratio have very little justification other than modelers' experience, and as a result, use of the index appears to be unwise and in decline (Kelloway, 1996).

Researchers also have reported the coefficient of determination for the model as an index of overall fit. Structural equation modeling programs typically report R^2 values for each endogenous variable as well as an overall coefficient of determination for the model. Although researchers have interpreted these indices as measures of model fit, they clearly do not address the question of whether the model can reproduce the covariance matrix. Rather, the model coefficient of determination and the R^2 values for individual endogenous variables are measures of variance accounted for, rather than measures of model fit (Medsker et al., 1994). It is quite possible to have a well-fitting model that explains only a modest amount of variance in the endogenous variables.

With the exception of R^2 values, the indices discussed thus far assess whether or not the model as a whole provides an adequate fit to the data. More detailed information can be acquired from tests of specific parameters composing the model. James and colleagues (1982) describe two types of statistical tests used in structural equation modeling; Condition 9 and Condition 10 tests. A Condition 10 test assesses the overidentifying restrictions placed on the model. The most common example of a Condition 10 test is the χ^2 likelihood test for goodness of fit. Using the term "test" loosely to include fit indices with unknown distributions, the fit indices discussed above would also qualify as Condition 10 tests.

In contrast, Condition 9 tests are tests of the specific parameters composing the model. Programs such as LISREL commonly report both the parameter and the standard error of estimate for that parameter. The ratio of the parameter to its standard error is also reported as a t test. In practice, however, and given the large sample sizes involved in structural equation modeling, these t values are interpreted using the critical values for the Z test. That is, values above 1.96 are significant at the $p < .05$ level. A Condition 9 test, therefore, assesses whether parameters predicted to be nonzero in the structural equation model are in fact significantly different from zero.

Again, it is important to note that consideration of the individual parameters composing the model is important for assessing the accuracy of the model. The parameter tests are not, in and of themselves, tests of model fit. Two likely results in testing structural equation models are that (a) a proposed model fits the data even though some parameters are nonsignificant and/or (b) a proposed model fits the data but some of the specified parameters are significant and opposite in direction to that predicted. In either case, the researcher's theory is disconfirmed even though the model may provide a good absolute fit to the data. The fit of the model has nothing to say about the validity of the individual predictions composing the model. One must move beyond the assessment of global fit to truly evaluate the results of structural equation modeling (Jöreskog, 1993).

Comparative Fit

Perhaps because of the problems inherent in assessing the absolute fit of a model to the data, researchers increasingly have turned to the assessment of comparative fit. The question of comparative fit deals with whether the model under consideration is better than some competing model. For example, many of the indices discussed below are based on choosing a model as a "baseline" and comparing the fit of theoretically derived models to the baseline model.

In some sense, all tests of model fit are based on a comparison of models. The tests discussed previously implicitly compare the theoretical model against the just-identified model. Recall that the just-identified model consists of all possible recursive paths between the variables. As a result, the model has 0 degrees of freedom (because the number of estimated paths is the same as the number of elements in the covariance matrix) and always provides a perfect fit to the data.

Indices of comparative fit are based on the opposite strategy. Rather than comparing against a model that provides a perfect fit to the data,

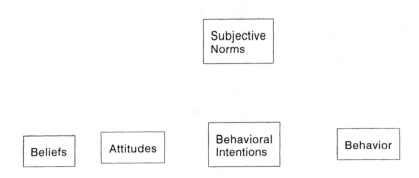

Figure 3.2.

indices of comparative fit typically choose as the baseline a model that is known a priori to provide a poor fit to the data. The most common baseline model is the "null" or "independence" model (the two terms are used interchangeably; LISREL printouts refer to the independence model, but much of the literature makes reference to the null model). The null model is a model that specifies no relationships between the variables composing the model. That is, if one were to draw the path model for the null model, it would have no paths connecting the variables (see Figure 3.2).

For example, Bentler and Bonett (1980) have suggested a normed fit index (NFI), defined as

$$(\chi^2_{indep} - \chi^2_{model})/\chi^2_{indep}$$

The NFI ranges from 0 to 1, with values exceeding 0.9 indicating a good fit.[1] As Bentler and Bonett (1980) point out, the NFI indicates the percentage improvement in fit over the baseline independence model. Thus, an NFI of 0.90 means that the model is 90% better fitting than the null model. Although the NFI is widely used, it may underestimate the fit of the model in small samples.

The nonnormed fit index (NNFI) uses a similar logic but adjusts the normed fit index for the number of degrees of freedom in the model. The NNFI is given by

$$(\chi^2_{indep} - df_{indep}/df_{model}\,\chi^2_{model})/(\chi^2_{indep} - df_{model})$$

Although this correction reduces the problem of underestimating fit, it introduces a new complication in that it may result in numbers outside of the 0 to 1 range. That is, the NNFI results in numbers with a lower bound of 0 but an upper bound greater than 1. Higher values of the NNFI indicate a better fitting model, and it is common to apply the 0.90 rule as indicating a good fit to the data.

Bollen's (1989) incremental fit index (IFI) reintroduces the scaling factor, so that IFI values range between 0 and 1, with higher values indicating a better fit to the data. The IFI is given by

$$(\chi^2_{indep} - \chi^2_{model})/(\chi^2_{indep} - df_{model})$$

Bentler (1990) proposed a comparative fit index (CFI) based on the noncentral χ^2 distribution. The CFI also ranges between 0 and 1, with values exceeding 0.90 indicating a good fit to the data. The CFI is based on the noncentrality parameter, which can be estimated as $\chi^2 - df$. Thus, the CFI is given by

$$1 - [(\chi^2_{model} - df_{model})/(\chi^2_{indep} - df_{indep})]$$

Marsh and colleagues (1988) proposed a relative fit index (RFI) defined as

$$\frac{(\chi^2_{indep} - \chi^2_{model}) - [df_{indep} - (df_{model}/n)]}{\chi^2_{indep} - (df_{indep}/n)}$$

Again, the RFI ranges between 0 and 1, with values approaching unity indicating a good fit to the data. The use of 0.90 as an indicator of a well-fitting model is also appropriate with this index.

Finally, Cudeck and Browne (1983) suggested the use of the cross-validation index as a measure of comparative fit. Cross-validation of models is well established in other areas of statistics (e.g., regression analyses; Browne & Cudeck, 1993; Cudeck & Browne, 1983). Traditionally, cross-validation required two samples: a calibration sample and a validation sample. The procedure relied on fitting a model to the calibration sample and then evaluating the discrepancy between the covariance matrix implied by the model to the covariance matrix of the validation sample. If the discrepancy was small, then the model was judged to fit the data in that it cross-validated to other samples.

The obvious practical problem with this strategy is the requirement for two samples. Browne and Cudeck (1989) suggested a solution to the problem by estimating the expected value of the cross-validation index using only data from a single sample. Although the mathematics of the expected value of the cross-validation index (ECVI) will not be presented here (the reader is referred to the source material cited above), the ECVI is thought to estimate the expected discrepancy (i.e., difference between the implied and actual covariance matrices) over all possible calibration samples. The ECVI has a lower bound of zero but no upper bound. Smaller values indicate better-fitting models. In addition to the point estimate of the ECVI, LISREL provides both the confidence intervals for the estimate and the ECVI values for the independence (null) and saturated (just-identified) models.

Parsimonious Fit

Parsimonious fit indices are concerned primarily with the cost-benefit trade-off of fit and degrees of freedom. It is not surprising that several of the indices can be calculated by adjusting other indices of fit for model complexity. For example, James and colleagues (1982) have proposed the parsimonious normed fit index (PNFI), which adjusts the NFI for model parsimony. The PNFI is calculated as

$$(df_{model} / df_{indep}) \times NFI$$

Similarly, the parsimonious goodness-of-fit index (PGFI) adjusts the GFI for the degrees of freedom in the model and is calculated as

$$1 - (P/N) \times GFI$$

where P = the number of estimated parameters in the model and N = the number of data points.

Both the PNFI and the PGFI range from 0 to 1, with higher values indicating a more parsimonious fit. Unlike the other fit indices we have discussed, there is no standard for how "high" either index should be to indicate parsimonious fit. Indeed, neither the PNFI nor the PGFI will likely reach the 0.90 cutoff used for other fit indices. Rather, these indices are best used to compare two competing theoretical models; that is, they would calculate an index of parsimonious fit for each model and choose the model with the highest level of parsimonious fit.

The Akaike Information Criterion (AIC) and Consistent Akaike Information Criterion (CAIC) (Akaike, 1987; Bozdogan, 1987) are also measures of parsimonious fit that consider both the fit of the model and the number of estimated parameters. AIC is defined as

$$\chi^2_{model} - 2df_{model}$$

and CAIC is defined as

$$\chi^2_{model} - (\ln N + 1)df_{model}$$

where N is the number of observations. For both indices, smaller values indicate a more parsimonious model. Neither index, however, is scaled to range between 0 and 1, and there are no conventions or guidelines to indicate what "small" means. Like the PNFI and PGFI, interpretation of the AIC and CAIC is based on comparing competing models and choosing the model that shows the most parsimony. McDonald and Marsh (1990) note that following this strategy using the AIC might result in overly complex models (i.e., although the AIC adjusts for parsimony, the adjustment is not sufficient to overcome a bias in favor of more complex models).

Nested Model Comparisons

As should be apparent at this point, the assessment of model fit is not a straightforward task. Indeed, from the discussion thus far, it should be clear that there are at least three views of what "model fit" means:

1. the absolute fit of the model to the data,
2. the fit of a model to the data relative to other models, or
3. the degree of parsimonious fit of the model relative to other models.

Given the problems inherent in assessing model fit, it is commonly suggested that models of interest be tested against reasonable alternative models. If we cannot show that our model fits the data perfectly, we can at least demonstrate that our model fits better than some other reasonable model. Although this may sound suspiciously like the question of comparative fit, recall that indices of comparative fit are based on comparison with the independence model, which is purposely defined as a model that provides a poor fit to the data. In contrast, the procedures we are about to discuss are based on comparing two plausible models of the data.

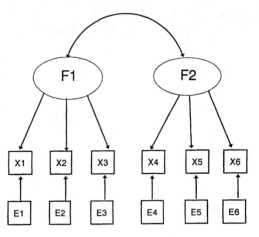

Figure 3.3.

Many such plausible and rival specifications exist. For example, consider the case of a confirmatory factor analysis model shown in Figure 3.3. The model suggests that there are two common factors, which are correlated, causing six indicators. Plausible rival hypotheses might include a model suggesting two orthogonal common factors (Figure 3.4) or a unidimensional model (Figure 3.5).

In the case of path analyses, an alternative specification of the Fishbein and Ajzen (1975) model might include the hypothesis that subjective norms about a behavior influence both attitudes and behavioral intentions (see Figure 3.6). Support for this modification has been

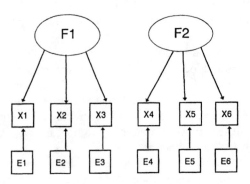

Figure 3.4.

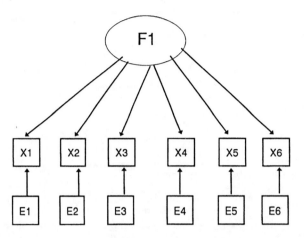

Figure 3.5.

found in some tests of Fishbein and Ajzen-based models (e.g., Fullagar, McCoy, & Shull, 1992; Kelloway & Barling, 1993). Although we are always interested in whether the model(s) fit the data absolutely, we also may be interested in which of these competing specifications provides the best fit to the data.

If the alternative models are in hierarchical or nested relationships, then these model comparisons may be made directly. A nested relationship exists between two models if one can obtain the model with the fewest number of free parameters by constraining some or all of the parameters in the model with the largest number of free parameters.

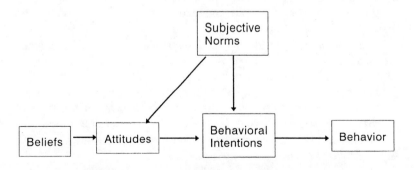

Figure 3.6.

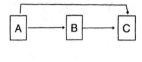

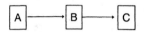

Figure 3.7.

That is, the model with the fewest parameters is a subset of the model with more parameters.

For example, consider two factor models of an eight-item test. Model A suggests that four items load on each factor and that the two factors are correlated (oblique). Model B suggests that the same four items load on each factor but that the two factors are orthogonal. In this case, Model B is nested in Model A. By taking Model A and constraining the interfactor correlation to equal 0, one obtains Model B. The nesting sequence results from the observation that Model B is composed of all the same parameters as Model A, with the exception of the interfactor correlation (which is not estimated in Model B).

Similarly, for a path model example, consider the model shown in Figure 3.7. The model at the top suggests that A predicts both B and C directly. In contrast, the model at the bottom suggests that A predicts B, which in turn predicts C. Again, these models stand in a nested sequence. By deleting the direct prediction of C from A from the first model, we obtain the second model (ergo, the second model is nested within the first).

When two models stand in a nested sequence, the difference between the two may be directly tested with the $\chi^2_{\text{difference}}$ test. The difference between the χ^2 values associated with each model is itself distributed as χ^2 with degrees of freedom equal to the difference in degrees of freedom for each model. For example, assume that the two-factor model with correlated factors generated $\chi^2(19) = 345.97$. Constraining the interfactor correlation between the two models to equal 0 results in $\chi^2(20) = 347.58$. The $\chi^2_{\text{difference}}$ is

$$347.58 - 345.97 = 1.61$$

which is distributed with

$$20 - 19 = 1 \text{ degree of freedom}$$

Because the critical value for χ^2 with 1 degree of freedom is 3.84 and the obtained value is less than the critical value, we conclude that there is no significant difference between the two models. By inference, then, the model hypothesizing two oblique factors is overly complex. That is, the additional parameter (the interfactor correlation) did not result in a significant increase in fit.

In this simple example, the models differ in only one parameter, and the results of the $\chi^2_{\text{difference}}$ test probably do not provide any information beyond the tests of individual parameters discussed at the beginning of this chapter. When models differ in more than one parameter, however, the $\chi^2_{\text{difference}}$ test is a useful omnibus test of the additional parameters that can be followed up by the Condition 9 tests of specific parameters.

Before leaving the subject of nested model comparisons, it is important to note that the test is valid only when the models stand in nested sequence. If the nesting sequence is not present, use of the $\chi^2_{\text{difference}}$ test is inappropriate. The key test of whether Model A is nested in Model B is whether all the relationships constituting Model A exist in Model B. That is, if Model B simply adds relationships to Model A, then the two models are nested. If there are other differences (e.g., Model B is obtained by deleting some parameters from Model A and adding some others), then the models are not nested.

Although the test is not conclusive, it should be apparent that given two models in nested sequence, the model with the fewest parameters will always provide the worst fit to the data (i.e., be associated with the highest χ^2 value and the larger degrees of freedom). Moreover, the degrees of freedom for the $\chi^2_{\text{difference}}$ test should always equal the number of additional paths contained in the more complex model.

Model Respecification

As noted earlier, perhaps no aspect of structural equation modeling techniques is more controversial than the role of model respecification. Despite the controversy (see, for example, Brannick, 1995; Kelloway, 1995; Williams, 1995), structural equation programs such as LISREL commonly provide the researcher with some guidelines for finding sources of model misspecification. That is, given that the proposed model does not fit the data, is there anything we can do to improve the fit of the model?

Two sources of information are particularly valuable. First, the tests of model parameters discussed at the beginning of this chapter provide some information about which parameters are contributing to the fit of the model and which parameters are not making such a contribution. Theory trimming (Pedhazur, 1982) is a common approach to model improvement. It essentially consists of deleting nonsignificant paths from the model to improve model fit.

Although these tests provide information about the estimated model parameters, LISREL also provides information about the nonestimated parameters. That is, the use of a theory-trimming approach asks, "What parameters can be deleted from the model?"; one can also adopt a theory-building approach that asks, "What parameters should be added to the model?"

These tests are technically known as Lagrange multiplier tests but are referred to in LISREL as the modification indices. For each parameter in the model that is set to zero, LISREL calculates the decrease in the model χ^2 that would be obtained from estimating that parameter. The amount of change in the model χ^2 is referred to as the modification index for that parameter.

Obviously, there is a trade-off between estimating more parameters (with the corresponding loss of degrees of freedom) and improving the fit of the model. Commonly, we would estimate any parameter that is associated with a modification index greater than 5.0; however, this rough guideline should be used with caution for several reasons.

First, recall that such specification searches are purely exploratory in nature. In contrast with the other parameters in the model, which are based on theory or previous research, parameters added on the basis of the modification indices (or, indeed, deleted on the basis of significance tests) may be reflecting sample-specific variance. The modifications made to the model following these procedures may not generalize to other samples.

Second, the process of theory trimming or theory building is analogous to the procedures of stepwise regression through either backward elimination (theory trimming) or forward entry (theory building). As such, both procedures are based on univariate procedures in which each parameter is considered in isolation. As a result, both theory trimming and theory building are based on a large number of statistical tests, with a corresponding inflation of Type I error rates. Moreover, the tests may be misleading in that adding a parameter to a model based on the modification indices may change the value of parameters already in the model (i.e., making theoretically based parameters nonsignificant).

Third, even when the modification indices are greater than 5.0, the improvement in model fit obtained from freeing parameters may be trivial to the model as a whole. For example, if the overall χ^2 for the model is 349.23, then it is questionable whether the improvement in fit (reduction of the χ^2 by 5.0) is worth the dangers of adding a parameter based on the modification indices.

Toward a Strategy for Assessing Model Fit

As has been evident throughout this discussion, the assessment of model fit is a complex question. Numerous fit indices have been proposed, each with a slightly different conception of what it means to say a model "fits the data." The literature is in agreement, however, on several fundamental points that provide the basis for a strategy of model testing.

First, the focus of assessing model fit almost invariably should be on comparing the fit of competing and theoretically plausible models. Simply stated, the available techniques for assessing model fit do a better job of contrasting models than they do of assessing one model in isolation. The researcher's task, then, is to generate plausible rival specifications and test them. Ideally, such rival specifications will consist of nested models allowing the use of direct methods of comparison such as the $\chi^2_{difference}$ test.

Second, and in a similar vein, rather than relying on modification indices and parameter tests to guide the development of models, researchers should be prepared a priori to identify and test the sources of ambiguity in their models. I elaborate on this theme in subsequent chapters, where examples of the major types of structural equation models are presented.

Third, given the varying definitions of model fit presented above, it is incumbent on researchers to use multiple measures of fit. As Loehlin (1987) notes, the use of multiple fit indices may place the researcher in the position of an individual with seven watches: If they all agree, then you know what time it is, but if they don't, you are no better off than if you had no watch. I suggest that the situation with regard to assessing model fit is not that serious. Understanding what each of the various fit indices means would suggest that, at a minimum, researchers would want to consider the issues of absolute fit, comparative fit, and parsimonious fit for each model tested. Fit indices therefore should be chosen so as to reflect each of these concerns (i.e., choosing one or two indices of each type of fit).

Finally, it is important for researchers to recognize that "model fit" does not equate to "truth" or "validity." The fit of a model is, at best, a necessary but not sufficient condition for the validity of the theory that generated the model predictions. Although the question of model fit is important, it is by no means the most important or only question we should ask about our data.

Note

1. Recall the previous discussion about the arbitrariness of such guidelines and the resultant need for cautious interpretation.

CHAPTER 4

Using LISREL

Having considered the general approach to be used in structural equation modeling, it is now time to consider the specifics of using LISREL to estimate and evaluate such models. It should be noted that other programs (e.g., EQS and EZPATH) are available to evaluate structural equation models. LISREL remains, however, a popular and widely available software package for structural equation modeling.

LISREL works by defining eight matrices; within each matrix are free and fixed parameters. Free parameters are unknowns to be estimated by the program, whereas fixed parameters are set to some predetermined value (usually zero).

For example, a typical LISREL matrix might contain three rows and two columns, as follows.

	K1	K2
X1	Free	Fixed
X2	Free	Fixed
X3	Fixed	Free

In this case, matrix elements (1, 1), (2, 1) and (3, 2) are going to be freely estimated by the program. Matrix elements (1, 2), (2, 2), and (3, 1) are fixed (set to zero). Researchers would specify the model to be tested by manipulating these matrices and whether their elements were fixed or free. Using the matrix formulation of LISREL, the researcher's task is to translate the model (i.e., the path diagram) into the LISREL matrices.

To do so, one has to understand what matrices are involved in the analyses and what forms they take.

The current release of LISREL (LISREL VIII) incorporates the SIMPLIS command language. Essentially, the SIMPLIS command language is an attempt to move away from the matrix formulation of the LISREL model and toward a more natural language approach to defining LISREL models. The researcher's task using the SIMPLIS language is to translate the model into SIMPLIS syntax.

We will focus on the matrix approach, rather than the SIMPLIS approach, to defining LISREL models. Although the reader is welcome to choose either approach to LISREL syntax, it should be noted that references to LISREL matrices continue to appear in the literature, and it is helpful to know the underlying structure of the program. Readers interested in using the SIMPLIS language are referred to Jöreskog and Sörbom (1992).

Whether one is using the matrix formulation or the SIMPLIS language, setting up a structural equation model in the LISREL environment involves three types of specification. First, you must tell LISREL how to read the data. Second, you have to specify the model to be estimated. Finally, you have to specify the type of output you want from your analysis.

The Matrix Formulation

To assist in the translation from path diagrams to matrices, it helps to remember a couple of points:

1. A *free* element in a LISREL matrix is the same as a path connecting the variables represented by the column and the row.
2. A *fixed* element in a LISREL path is the same as a hypothesis of no path between the variables represented by the column and the row.
3. To refer to the elements of a matrix, we always refer to the row, then the column [e.g., (1, 4) means the element in the first row and the fourth column].
4. In path diagrams, the direction of the relationship is given by the direction of the arrow. In LISREL matrices, columns always cause (predict) rows.

The LISREL model consists of the measurement model for the X (exogenous) variables, the measurement model for the Y (endogenous)

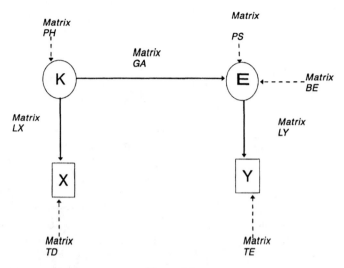

Figure 4.1.

variables, and the structural model, which relates the two. The full LISREL model comprises eight matrices (see Figure 4.1).

By specifying a subset of these matrices, the user can tailor LISREL to specific problems. For example, if you are interested in a factor analysis of the exogenous (X) variables, you need only be concerned with the **LX** (factor loadings; i.e., loadings of variables on common factors), **PH** (factor covariances or correlations), and **TD** (unique factors for each variable; i.e., residuals) matrices, which compose the measurement model for the exogenous variables (see Figure 4.2).

In the model, there are *NK* (*N* = number, *K* stands for latent variables on the exogenous side of the LISREL model) latent variables or factors. They are related through a series of paths (found in the **LX** matrix) to a series of *NX* (number of observed variables) observed variables/measures. The intercorrelations or covariances of the factors are contained in the matrix **PH**.

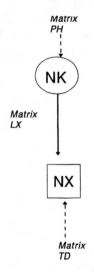

Figure 4.2.

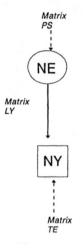

Figure 4.3.

The unique factors (residuals) for each observed variable are in matrix **TD**.

Similarly, the measurement model for the Y variables consists of the **LY** (factor loadings), **PS** (factor covariances), and **TE** (residuals) matrices (see Figure 4.3). There are NE (number of latent endogenous variables) latent variables or factors. They are related through a series of paths (found in the **LY** matrix) to a series of NY (number of observed endogenous variables) observed variables/measures). The intercorrelations or covariances of the factors are contained in the matrix **PS**. The unique factors (residuals) for each observed variable are in matrix **TE**.

The structural model relating exogenous (X) and endogenous (Y) variables consists of the **GA** (structural coefficients relating X to Y variables) and **BE** (structural coefficients relating Y to Y variables) matrices (see Figure 4.4).

NX observed variables are related (**GA** contains the path values) to NY observed variables. The endogenous (Y) observed variables may also predict other Y variables. These paths are found in the **BE** matrix. Finally, the unexplained variances (i.e., residuals) of the Y predicted variables are found in matrix **PS**.

Each of the eight matrices in LISREL can be thought of as a matrix of free and fixed values. A free value is an unknown, that is, a value that

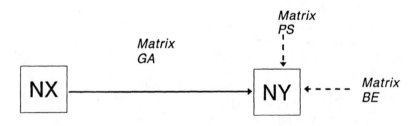

Figure 4.4.

TABLE 4.1 LISREL Matrices

Matrix	Order	Form	Alternates	Mode	Comments
1. LY	$NY \times NE$	FU	ID, IZ ,ZI, DI, FU	FI	Relates Ys to Es (factor loadings)
2. LX	$NX \times NK$	FU	ID, IZ, ZI, DI, FU	FI	Relates Xs to Ks (factor loadings)
3. BE	$NE \times NE$	ZE	ZE, SD, FU	FI	Relates Es to Es (structural coefficients)
4. GA	$NE \times NK$	FU	ID, IZ, ZI, DI, FU	FR	Relates Es to Ks (structural coefficients)
5. PH	$NK \times NK$	SY	ID, DI, SY, ST	FR	Relates Ks to Ks (factor covariances)
6. PS	$NE \times NE$	SY	ZE, DI, SY	FR	Residuals of Es (factor covariances in a factor analysis of Y variables or errors of prediction in a structural model)
7. TE	$NY \times NY$	DI	ZE, DI, SY	FR	Residuals of Ys (unique factors)
8. TD	$NX \times NX$	DI	ZE, DI, SY	FR	Residuals of Xs (unique factors)

NOTE: For Order, NX = number of observed exogenous (source) variables, NY = number of observed endogenous (downstream) variables, NK = number of latent exogenous variables, and NE = number of latent endogenous variables. For Forms, ZE = zero matrix (a matrix filled with zeros), ID = identity matrix (a zero matrix with 1s in the diagonal), IZ = partitioned identity and zero, ZI = partitioned zero and identity, DI = diagonal matrix (only the diagonal elements are stored), SD = subdiagonal matrix (elements below the diagonal), SY = symmetric matrix that is not diagonal (diagonal elements do not equal 1), ST = symmetric matrix with 1s in the diagonal (e.g., correlations), and FU = a rectangular or square nonsymmetric matrix. For modes, FI = fixed and FR = free.

you want LISREL to estimate for you. A fixed value is set to a predetermined value (often 0) and is not estimated by the program. Table 4.1 gives a summary of the eight matrices, their default forms, and the various alternate forms they can assume.

It's All Greek to Me!

To be totally fluent in LISREL, Hayduk (1987) suggests that we should know the Greek names for the LISREL matrices. This allows one to make puns such as "LISREL is all Greek to me." Should your taste in humor run along these lines, you may be interested to know that

$$
\begin{aligned}
\mathbf{LX} &= \text{Lambda X} \\
\mathbf{LY} &= \text{Lambda Y} \\
\mathbf{BE} &= \text{Beta} \\
\mathbf{GA} &= \text{Gamma} \\
\mathbf{PH} &= \text{Phi} \\
\mathbf{PS} &= \text{Psi} \\
\mathbf{TD} &= \text{Theta-Delta} \\
\mathbf{TE} &= \text{Theta-Epsilon}
\end{aligned}
$$

LISREL Keywords

The matrix form of LISREL operates through keywords that allow the user to specify the forms of the relevant matrices. For most commands, only the first two letters are necessary.

To run LISREL, you create a list of commands in which you

1. specify the data,
2. specify the model, and
3. specify the output.

LISREL command files often begin with an optional **TItle** statement. This command is optional but recommended. If used, LISREL will print the title throughout the output file, thereby providing the user with a means of documenting the analysis.

Specifying the Data

DAta

The **DAta** statement is used to define the data. The following may be specified:

$$
\begin{aligned}
\text{NGroups} &= \text{number of groups (default} = 1), \\
\text{NInpvar} &= \text{number of input variables (default} = 0), \\
\text{NObs} &= \text{number of observations,}
\end{aligned}
$$

XM = a missing value label (used when reading in raw data; by default, LISREL uses listwise deletion of missing values), and

MAtrix = the type of matrix to be analyzed. (Note that this is not necessarily the same type as the matrix that you read into LISREL. For example, you can request that LISREL read in a covariance matrix and then analyze the correlation matrix.)

MAs can assume the following values:

MM = matrix of moments about 0,

CM = a covariance matrix (default),

KM = a correlation matrix,

AM = an augmented moment matrix,

OM = a correlation matrix of optimal scores produced by PRELIS, or

PM = a matrix of polychoric or polyserial correlations.

For example, a typical DAta statement might look like:

```
DA NI = 10 NO = 100 MA = CM.
```

LISREL will read the statement as saying that you have 10 variables (NI = 10) and 100 observations (NO = 100), and you want the analyses to be based on the covariance matrix (MA = CM).

LAbels

The **LAbel** statement is used to assign labels to the variables being read. Although LISREL will read LAbels from an external file, I've typically found it useful to include the labels in the command file.

A typical LAbel statement might look like this:

```
LA
     'Label 1' 'Label 2' 'Label 3'
```

Note that LISREL expects to read as many labels as the number of input variables specified on the DAta statement.

If you only want to label some of the variables, then you can use a "/" to terminate reading the labels. For example:

```
DA NI = 10 NO = 200 MA = CM
LA
'Behavior' 'Intentions' 'Norms' 'Attitudes' 'Beliefs'/
```

The DAta statement tells LISREL to read 10 variables, but labels are provided for only the first five variables.

RAw Data

The **RAw data** statement is used when you want to read raw data into the LISREL program. It is typically followed by both (a) the filename in which the raw data are stored and (b) a Fortran variable format statement (if not contained in the data file).

For example:

```
RA FI= data.dat FO
(5F7.3)
```

tells LISREL that the raw data are found in the file called "data.dat" and that the next line in the command file is the Fortran variable definition statement (in this case specifying five variables in fields of seven columns with three places behind the decimal). The Fortran format statement may be replaced by an asterisk (*) indicating that the data are in free format (i.e., separated by columns or spaces).

CM, KM, MM, OM, and PM

These commands tell LISREL to read a specified matrix using the conventions described earlier (e.g., **CM** = covariance matrix). In addition to the type of matrix, you must specify the form of the matrix, either symmetrical (elements including and below the diagonal, SY) or full (all elements in the matrix, FU). For example, to read in a correlation matrix, you might write

```
KM SY
 1.00
  .50  1.00
  .40   .30  1.00
```

You also can use the FI command (as described earlier) to read the matrix from an external file.

ME and SD Commands. These commands read in a vector of either means (**ME**) or standard deviations (**SD**). Again, the FI command may be used to read data from an external file. Given our earlier focus on analysis of the covariance matrix, it is useful to note that given a correlation matrix, a vector of means, and a vector of standard deviations, LISREL can compute the covariance matrix prior to analysis.

SElect

The **SElect** command is used to reorder the variables in the matrix. This is a useful feature because LISREL expects to read the endogenous variables first, followed by the exogenous variables. You also can use the SElect command to drop variables from the analysis. For example, given that you have read in six input variables, the statement

```
SE
   6 5 4 3 2 1
```

reverses the order of the variables, while

```
SE
   6 5 4 2 1/
```

both reorders the variables and deletes the third variable from the analysis. Note that the "/" is used to terminate variable selection before the number of input variables is reached.

Specifying the Model

The LISREL model specification commands follow the data in the command file. Models are specified using the **MOdel** command. You can specify

NY = number of observed endogenous variables,
NX = number of observed exogenous variables,
NE = number of latent endogenous variables, or
NK = number of latent exogenous variables.

Specifying a subset of these parameters will result in specification of a LISREL submodel. For example, if you specify

NK and NX:	You are doing a factor analysis of exogenous variables involving matrices **LX, PH,** and **TD.**
NE and NY:	You are doing a factor analysis of endogenous variables involving matrices **LY, PS,** and **TE.**
NX and NY:	You are doing a path model using only observed variables and involving matrices **BE, GA,** and **PS.**
NX, NY, NK, and NE:	You are doing a full latent variable model using all eight of the LISREL matrices.

For each matrix involved in the model selected, you can either use the default form (see Table 4.1 on page 45) or specify an alternate form with the MOdel command. You specify an alternate form by typing (on the same line as the MOdel command)

```
MN = AA, BB
```

where MN = a name of a parameter matrix,
AA = a valid alternate form for that matrix, and
BB = either FIxed or FRee.

In general, LISREL is set up so that the default forms of each parameter matrix are the ones most often used. You can modify the default forms by (a) selecting a new form as shown above or (b) modifying the **FIxed/FRee** status of individual elements of a parameter matrix. To modify these elements, you use the FR and FI commands. For example:

FIx LX(1,2) LX(2,2)

modifies two elements in the **LX** matrix by setting them to be a fixed value. The modified elements are located at matrix coordinates (1, 2) and (2, 2).

Similarly,

FRee LX(1,2) LX(2,2)

modifies the same two elements by setting them as free (to be estimated values). In addition to setting elements to be FRee or FIxed, you also can set them up to be EQual to another element. Each group of elements that are constrained to be equal are defined on a separate **EQ** command. For example:

EQ LY(3,4) LY(4,4) BE(2,1) GA(4,6)

defines all the listed elements as being equal to the same value. Typically, the first element listed will be a free parameter—LISREL will estimate the free parameter and set the remaining values to be equal to it.

The **VAlue** and **STarting value** commands are used to define nonzero values for fixed parameters and to set the starting values for free parameters. The commands are equivalent and can be used interchangeably. For example:

VA 1.5 LX(2,1) LY(6,2) GA (1,2)

assigns the value 1.5 to the listed elements. If the elements are fixed, this becomes an assigned value; if they're free, it becomes a start value.

The **LE** and **LK** commands are used to supply labels for the latent endogenous (LE) and latent exogenous (LK) variables. The format for these commands is exactly the same as for the LA command described earlier.

Specifying the Output

The user can specify the amount and quality of LISREL output by using the **OUtput** subcommand. You specify the estimation method by one of the following keywords:

IV = instrumental variable method,

TS = two-stage least squares,

UL = unweighted least squares,

GL = generalized least squares,

ML = maximum likelihood (this is the default),

WL = generally weighted least squares, or

DL = diagonally weighted least squares.

Additional options provided by LISREL are

RC = ridge constant: matrix will be multiplied repeatedly by 10 until the matrix becomes positive definite;

SL = significance of modification procedures expressed as a percentage (see AM below);

NS = do not compute starting values (must be supplied by the user);

RO = ridge option: used with RC, invoked automatically if the covariance matrix is not positive definite;

AM = automatic model modification: LISREL will automatically modify the model by sequentially freeing the fixed parameter with the largest modification index; and

SO = scaling check off: turns off LISREL's capacity to check for scale assignment to latent variables.

LISREL always provides standard output consisting of the information you provide, the initial estimates, the LISREL estimates (ML or UL), and the overall goodness-of-fit measures. Additional output can be requested by the following keywords:

SE = standard errors;

TV = t values;

PC = correlations of estimates;

RS = residuals, normalized residuals, and Q plot;

EF = total effects and indirect effects;

MR = miscellaneous results, equivalent to RS, EF, and VA;

MI = modification indices;
FS = factor scores regressions;
SS = standardized solution;
SC = solution completely standardized;
AL = print everything;
TO = print 80 characters/line (normal printer);
WP = print 132 characters/line (wide carriage printer); and
ND = number of decimals (0-8) in printed output.

LISREL also allows you to save specified matrices to external files at termination. The required syntax is

```
OU matrix name = file
```

where matrix name can be LY, LX, BE, GA, PH, PS, TE, TD, TY, TX, AL, or KA. In addition, LISREL will allow you to save the following matrices:

MA = reordered input matrix,
SI = sigma (implied covariance matrix),
RM = regression matrix of latent on observed variables (factor scores), and
EC = estimated asymptotic covariance matrix of LISREL estimates.

Finally, several commands allow you to control the iterative procedure used by LISREL. You can specify

TM = maximum number of CPU seconds allowed for current problem (e.g., TM = 60);
IT = maximum number of iterations (default is 3 × number of free parameters);
AD = check the admissibility of the solution after m iterations, and stop the procedure if the check fails (e.g., AD = 10); and
EP = convergence criterion (epsilon); a default value (EP = .000001) usually results in a solution accurate to three decimal places.

CHAPTER 5 Confirmatory Factor Analysis

In this chapter, we consider the operationalization of a measurement model through confirmatory factor analysis. As will become apparent, applications of confirmatory factor analysis are particularly appropriate when there is a debate about the dimensionality or factor structure of a scale or measure. In this chapter, we consider the dimensionality of a measure of union commitment.

Since the original publication of the Gordon, Philpot, Burt, Thompson, and Spiller (1980) 30-item union commitment scale, there have been numerous factor analytic studies of the scale (e.g., Friedman & Harvey, 1986; Fullagar, 1986; Kelloway, Catano, & Southwell, 1992; Klandermans, 1990). Kelloway and colleagues (1992) proposed a shorter 13-item version of the scale designed to represent three factors: Union Loyalty; Willingness to Work for the Union; and Responsibility to the Union.

In this chapter, we will conduct a confirmatory factor analysis of the shortened scale based on data drawn from 217 union stewards. In developing and conducting the analysis, we will follow Bollen and Long's (1993) description of structural equation modeling as comprising five steps:

1. model specification,
2. identification,
3. estimation,
4. testing fit, and
5. respecification.

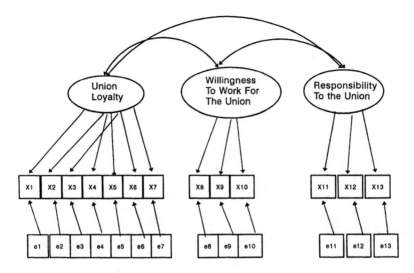

Figure 5.1.

Model Specification

The first step in operationalizing the model was to clarify exactly what relationships the model proposed. Figure 5.1 presents the proposed model. Note that the first factor (Union Loyalty) is measured by seven items, the second (Willingness to Work for the Union) by three items, and the third (Responsibility to the Union) by three items. Note also that each observed variable is also caused by a second latent variable representing the residual (or unique factors for factor analysts). Finally, each of the three factors is allowed to correlate with the other latent variables (i.e., the factors are oblique).

Given our focus on comparing models, it is appropriate to develop rival models to contrast with the proposed three-factor solutions. As noted earlier, ideally these rival models will stand in nested sequence with the model of interest to allow for the use of direct comparisons with the $\chi^2_{\text{difference}}$ test. The best source of such rival specification is the literature. In the case of the union commitment scale, for example, Friedman and Harvey (1986) reanalyzed the data from Gordon and colleagues (1980) and suggested a two-factor solution, with one factor representing attitudes and the other representing behavioral intentions.

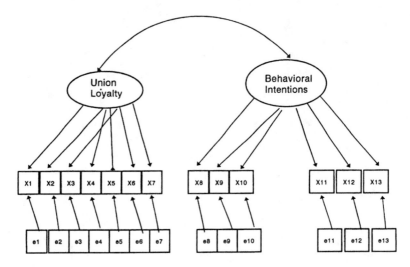

Figure 5.2.

For the current example, the two-factor model is depicted in Figure 5.2. Essentially, one obtains the two-factor model by combining the Willingness to Work for the Union and Responsibility to the Union factors. Although it is not intuitively obvious, the two-factor model is nested within the three-factor model. That is, by fixing the correlation between Willingness and Responsibility to equal 1.0, you obtain the two-factor model from the original three-factor model. The $\chi^2_{\text{difference}}$ test therefore will have 2 degrees of freedom (because there will be two fewer intercorrelations estimated).

If the literature does not provide a reasonable alternative to the factor structure you hypothesize, alternative structures may be obtained by constraining one or more parameters in the original model. In general, for any model that contains a number of correlated factors, nested models may be obtained by estimating (a) a model containing orthogonal factors (i.e., constraining all interfactor correlations to equal zero, see Figure 5.3) and/or (b) a unidimensional model (i.e., constraining all interfactor correlations to equal 1.0, see Figure 5.4).

From Pictures to LISREL

The model thought to explain the observed correlations between the union commitment items implies a set of structural equations. In the

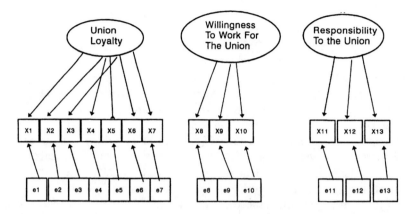

Figure 5.3.

LISREL environment, you do not have to worry about the exact form of the equations, but you do have to be concerned with the form of the relevant matrices. The process of translating the models into LISREL analyses is similar for all models, so we will focus on the three-factor model as an example.

Before beginning the process of translating the figures into LISREL commands, it is important to note that LISREL allows you to conduct confirmatory factor analyses on both the exogenous (i.e., using matrices **LX**, **PH**, and **TD**) and endogenous (i.e., using matrices **LY**, **PS**, and **TE**)

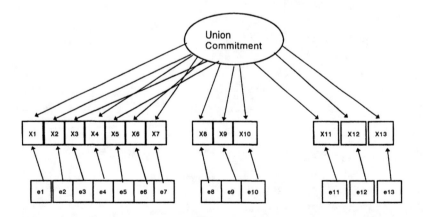

Figure 5.4.

sides of the full model. The choice of which side of the model to use is largely left to the user. As will become apparent, there are some advantages to using the exogenous (X) side of the model, but the numerical results should be exactly the same whichever side is used.

Because this is a factor analysis (for convenience only, of the exogenous variables), there are three matrices to be concerned with: **LX** (factor loadings), **PH** (interfactor correlations), and **TD** (unique factors). The **LX** matrix will have three columns (one for each latent variable) and 14 rows (one for each item). The **PH** matrix will have three columns and three rows and will be symmetrical (i.e., the elements above the diagonal will be the same as the elements below the diagonal because it is a correlation matrix). Finally, the **TD** matrix will be a vector (one row) with 14 columns (representing the 14 unique factors). The complete specification for the three matrices (indicating which elements are FRee or FIxed) is given below.

There are 29 parameters to be estimated (13 factor loadings + 13 unique factors + 3 interfactor correlations). With 13 variables, this implies a number of degrees of freedom for the model equal to

$$13 \times (13 + 1)/2 - 29 = 62.$$

Following the matrix presentations, I have enclosed the annotated code used to test the model. Note the correspondence between the code and the matrix forms presented.

```
        LX MATRIX
        K1    K2    K3
  X1    FR    FI    FI
  X2    FR    FI    FI
  X3    FR    FI    FI
  X4    FR    FI    FI
  X5    FR    FI    FI
  X6    FR    FI    FI
  X7    FR    FI    FI
  X8    FI    FR    FI
  X9    FI    FR    FI
  X10   FI    FR    FI
  X11   FI    FI    FR
  X12   FI    FI    FR
  X13   FI    FI    FR
```

```
PHI MATRIX
        K1    K2    K3
K1     1.00
K2     FR    1.00
K3     FR    FR    1.00

TD MATRIX
X1    X2    X3    X4    X5    X6    X7    X8    X9    X10
FR    FR    FR    FR    FR    FR    FR    FR    FR    FR
X11   X12   X13
FR    FR    FR
ANNOTATED CODE
TI  Confirmatory Factor Analysis of the Union Commitment
    Scale
```

Note: The title is optional but recommended.

```
DA  NI = 13 NO = 217 MA = CM
```

Note: There are 13 input variables (items), with 217 respondents, and I want to analyze the covariance matrix (CM).

```
ME
3.922   4.336   3.940   3.811   4.198   4.479   4.101
4.083   4.221   4.060   4.171   3.899   3.820
```

Note: This is the vector of means for each item.

```
SD
.937    .856    .991    .921    .851    .714    .917
.878    .837    .987    .846    .976   1.050
```

Note: This is the vector of standard deviations for each item.

```
KM FU
    1.000    .443    .643    .621    .635    .423    .564
     .531    .370    .331    .542    .497    .550
     .443   1.000    .531    .421    .480    .432    .504
     .351    .283    .288    .476    .323    .371
```

```
 .643   .531  1.000   .510   .634   .414   .485
 .405   .368   .359   .448   .343   .426
 .621   .421   .510  1.000   .698   .392   .615
 .529   .367   .339   .511   .452   .616
 .635   .480   .634   .698  1.000   .468   .603
 .529   .361   .388   .551   .426   .553
 .423   .432   .414   .392   .468  1.000   .427
 .549   .604   .577   .477   .369   .406
 .564   .504   .485   .615   .603   .427  1.000
 .455   .314   .372   .532   .441   .634
 .531   .351   .405   .529   .529   .549   .455
1.000   .561   .571   .392   .302   .413
 .370   .283   .368   .367   .361   .604   .314
 .561  1.000   .629   .391   .288   .377
 .331   .288   .359   .339   .388   .577   .372
 .571   .629  1.000   .370   .309   .382
 .542   .476   .448   .511   .551   .477   .532
 .392   .391   .370  1.000   .727   .712
 .497   .323   .343   .452   .426   .369   .441
 .302   .288   .309   .727  1.000   .710
 .550   .371   .426   .616   .553   .406   .634
 .413   .377   .382   .712   .710  1.000
```

Note: This is the full correlation matrix.

```
MO NX = 13 NK = 3 PH = ST
```

Note: The first line of the model command defines 13 X variables and three K variables, thereby specifying a factor analysis model using matrices **TD**, **LX**, and **PH**. "PH = ST" indicates that the interfactor covariance matrix is the lower part of a symmetric matrix and has 1s in the diagonal; hence, it is a correlation matrix—the off-diagonal elements contain the disattenuated (corrected for unreliability) correlations between the three latent variables (factors). The ST form is a convenience provided by the LISREL authors for confirmatory factor analysis. It applies only to analyses using the exogenous side of the LISREL model.

```
FR LX(1,1) LX(2,1) LX(3,1) LX(4,1) LX(5,1) LX(6,1)
```

```
FR LX(7,1)
```

Note: Here I define the first factor by telling LISREL to freely estimate the loadings of the first seven variables (seven Union Loyalty items) on the first factor.

```
FR LX(8,2) LX(9,2) LX(10,2)
```

Note: These lines define the second factor by telling LISREL to freely estimate the loadings for the next three variables (three Willingness to Work for the Union items) on the second factor (Willingness).

```
FR LX(11,3) LX(12,3) LX(13,3)
```

Note: Left as an exercise for the reader. It may help you to know that the Responsibility to the Union scale has three items.

```
OU ML SC TV
```

Note: The output command tells LISREL that I want a maximum likelihood solution (ML). I also want LISREL to provide the completely standardized solution for the estimated parameters (SC) and the *t* values (significance tests) for the parameters.

Additional Comments

You will note that I did not have to specify the FIxed elements in the LX matrix. This is because the default form of the matrix is full (*NX* rows × *NK* columns), and all elements are fixed. To specify the loadings I want, therefore, I only have to free the elements I want estimated.

By declaring the **PH** matrix to be ST, I have declared the matrix to be symmetrical, with 1s in the diagonal and free elements in the off-diagonals. No further specification is necessary to produce the correlation matrix I want. The ST specification is a convenience provided by the authors of LISREL for doing confirmatory factor analysis. It applies only to the **PH** matrix and can be used only for a factor analysis of the exogenous variables.

Because this command sets 1s in the diagonals of the factor covariance matrix, and because the diagonals of **PH** represent the variances of the latent variables, using the PH = ST specification tells LISREL that latent variables are in standard score form. In effect, the specification assigns a metric (i.e., a scale of measurement) to the latent variables. Recall that latent variables are, by definition, not directly measured. Unless the user indicates a scale of measurement for the latent variables, LISREL will not be able to estimate a solution.

Although the PH = ST specification is a convenience provided for confirmatory factor analyses, there is another way to set the scale of measurement for latent variables. That is, you can tell LISREL that the latent variable uses the same scale of measurement as one of the observed variables. Although this is the method typically used when conducting confirmatory factor analysis on the endogenous (Y) side of the model, it works equally well on the exogenous (X) side.

For example, you can set the scale of measurement for an endogenous latent variable by FIxing an element of the LY matrix to equal 1. For example:

```
VA 1.0 LY(1,1)
   FI LY(1,1)
```

These lines tell LISREL that the first factor is on the same scale as the first variable.

TD by default is diagonal (a vector of one row by NX columns) with all free elements. Because this is what I want, no further specification is necessary. Conceptually, the form of the TD matrix represents the assumption that error variances (unique factors) are uncorrelated. Although this assumption is universal in the psychological literature on factor analysis, it is not required by LISREL.

Identification

For confirmatory factor analyses, issues of model identification typically are dealt with by default. That is, in most applications of confirmatory factor analysis, the latent variables or factors are hypothesized to "cause" the observed variables. In such applications, the model is recursive in that the causal flow is expected to be from the latent variables to the observed variables.

Although this formulation of the measurement model is the most common, it is important to note that Bollen and Lennox (1991) have recently pointed out that it is not a necessary formulation. Specifically,

Bollen and Lennox (1991) distinguish between the use of "effect" indicators (those that are caused by latent variables) and "causal" indicators (those that cause latent variables). Although recognition of this distinction may have substantial implications for how organizational researchers test hypotheses about measurement relations, the implementation of "causal" indicator measurement models is not straightforward (MacCallum & Browne, 1993) and the Bollen and Lennox (1991) formulation has not yet seen widespread application in the research literature. In any event, reliance on the common factor model as the basis for confirmatory factor analyses implicitly assumes a one-way causal flow. The second overidentifying condition is the imposition of the constraint that at least some factor loadings are 0.

Bollen (1989) summarizes the issue of model identification in confirmatory factor analyses by citing three rules for model identification. As previously discussed, the "t rule" suggests that the number of estimated parameters be less than the number of nonredundant elements in the covariance matrix. Bollen (1989) also indicates that confirmatory factor analyses models are identified if (a) there are at least three indicators (observed variables) for each latent variable (factor) or (b) there are at least two indicators for each latent variable and the factors are allowed to correlate (i.e., an oblique solution). Both the two-indicator and three-indicator rules assume that the unique factor loadings (i.e., error terms) are uncorrelated.

Although the three-indicator rule is perhaps the most commonly cited, the empirical evidence supports the use of two indicators for each latent variable when the sample size is large. Specifically, in their Monte Carlo study, Anderson and Gerbing (1984) found that with small samples (e.g., $n < 100$), the use of only two indicators for each latent variable led to both convergence failures and improper solutions for confirmatory factor analyses. Using three indicators for each latent variable and sample sizes above 200 almost eliminated both convergence failures and the occurrence of improper solutions.

Estimation

The following is a sample of the type of output you obtain from LISREL. The output is divided into a number of sections. First, LISREL echoes the model specifications you entered and displays each matrix involved in the model in its specified form. Freely estimated parameters are numbered consecutively.

The next section of output is the maximum likelihood estimates provided by LISREL. These are the unstandardized estimates (comparable to unstandardized regression weights) and should be interpreted in the light of the scales on which the variables are measured. LISREL then presents the fit indices for the model. The R^2 values for each variable are indications of how well the latent variables explain the variance in the observed variables. The fit indices are then presented, followed by the optional output you have requested. Following is the annotated output for the three-factor union commitment model previously presented.

```
Ti Confirmatory Factor Analysis of the Union Commitment Scale
NUMBER OF INPUT VARIABLES  13
NUMBER OF Y - VARIABLES      0
NUMBER OF X - VARIABLES     13
NUMBER OF ETA - VARIABLES    0
NUMBER OF KSI - VARIABLES    3
NUMBER OF OBSERVATIONS     217
```

Note: This is a useful check to make sure LISREL is reading the model the way you intended. The commands specify 13 X variables and 3 k variables (factors). There are 217 observations.

```
Ti Confirmatory Factor Analysis of the Union Commitment Scale
COVARIANCE MATRIX TO BE ANALYZED
```

	VAR 1	VAR 2	VAR 3	VAR 4	VAR 5	VAR 6
VAR 1	0.88					
VAR 2	0.36	0.73				
VAR 3	0.60	0.45	0.98			
VAR 4	0.54	0.33	0.47	0.85		
VAR 5	0.51	0.35	0.53	0.55	0.72	
VAR 6	0.28	0.26	0.29	0.26	0.28	0.51
VAR 7	0.48	0.40	0.44	0.52	0.47	0.28
VAR 8	0.44	0.26	0.35	0.43	0.40	0.34
VAR 9	0.29	0.20	0.31	0.28	0.26	0.36
VAR 10	0.31	0.24	0.35	0.31	0.33	0.41
VAR 11	0.43	0.34	0.38	0.40	0.40	0.29

| VAR 12 | 0.45 | 0.27 | 0.33 | 0.41 | 0.35 | 0.26 |
| VAR 13 | 0.54 | 0.33 | 0.44 | 0.60 | 0.49 | 0.30 |

COVARIANCE MATRIX TO BE ANALYZED

	VAR 7	VAR 8	VAR 9	VAR 10	VAR 11	VAR 12
VAR 7	0.84					
VAR 8	0.37	0.77				
VAR 9	0.24	0.41	0.70			
VAR 10	0.34	0.49	0.52	0.97		
VAR 11	0.41	0.29	0.28	0.31	0.72	
VAR 12	0.39	0.26	0.24	0.30	0.60	0.95
VAR 13	0.61	0.38	0.33	0.40	0.63	0.73

COVARIANCE MATRIX TO BE ANALYZED

	VAR 13
VAR 13	1.10

Ti Confirmatory Factor Analysis of the Union Commitment Scale
PARAMETER SPECIFICATIONS

LAMBDA-X

	KSI 1	KSI 2	KSI 3
VAR 1	1	0	0
VAR 2	2	0	0
VAR 3	3	0	0
VAR 4	4	0	0
VAR 5	5	0	0
VAR 6	6	0	0
VAR 7	7	0	0
VAR 8	0	8	0
VAR 9	0	9	0
VAR 10	0	10	0
VAR 11	0	0	11
VAR 12	0	0	12
VAR 13	0	0	13

PHI

	KSI 1	KSI 2	KSI 3
KSI 1	0		
KSI 2	14	0	
KSI 3	15	16	0

THETA-DELTA

VAR 1	VAR 2	VAR 3	VAR 4	VAR 5	VAR 6
17	18	19	20	21	22

THETA-DELTA

VAR 7	VAR 8	VAR 9	VAR 10	VAR 11	VAR 12
23	24	25	26	27	28

THETA-DELTA

VAR 13
29

Note: LISREL tells you what parameters are freely estimated and numbers them consecutively. This is a useful to check that you have specified the model correctly.

```
Ti Confirmatory Factor Analysis of the Union Commitment
Scale

OUTPUT =   Number of Iterations = 8
LISREL ESTIMATES (MAXIMUM LIKELIHOOD)

LAMBDA-X
```

	KSI 1	KSI 2	KSI 3
VAR 1	0.73	- -	- -
	(0.05)		
	13.37		
VAR 2	0.52	- -	- -
	(0.05)		
	9.54		
VAR 3	0.71	- -	- -
	(0.06)		
	11.87		
VAR 4	0.72	- -	- -
	(0.05)		
	13.37		
VAR 5	0.70	- -	- -
	(0.05)		
	14.43		
VAR 6	0.43	- -	- -
	(0.05)		
	9.48		

VAR 7	0.68	- -	- -
	(0.05)		
	12.45		
VAR 8	- -	0.69	- -
		(0.05)	
		12.68	
VAR 9	- -	0.63	- -
		(0.05)	
		11.84	
VAR 10	- -	0.75	- -
		(0.06)	
		11.97	
VAR 11	- -	- -	0.73
			(0.05)
			15.23
VAR 12	- -	- -	0.80
			(0.06)
			14.04
VAR 13	- -	- -	0.90
			(0.06)
			15.16

PHI

	KSI 1	KSI 2	KSI 3
KSI 1	1.00		
KSI 2	0.72	1.00	
	(0.05)		
	15.96		
KSI 3	0.78	0.56	1.00
	(0.04)	(0.06)	
	21.78	9.42	

THETA-DELTA

VAR 1	VAR 2	VAR 3	VAR 4	VAR 5	VAR 6
0.34	0.46	0.47	0.33	0.23	0.32
(0.04)	(0.05)	(0.05)	(0.04)	(0.03)	(0.03)
8.83	9.82	9.34	8.83	8.30	9.83

THETA-DELTA

VAR 7	VAR 8	VAR 9	VAR 10	VAR 11	VAR 12
0.37	0.29	0.31	0.42	0.19	0.32
(0.04)	(0.04)	(0.04)	(0.06)	(0.03)	(0.04)
9.17	6.89	7.69	7.57	6.81	7.94

THETA-DELTA
VAR 13
———
  0.29
(0.04)
  6.89

Note: For each estimated parameter, LISREL provides the unstandardized maximum likelihood estimate, the standard error of the estimate (in brackets), and the t value associated with the estimate (i.e., the estimate divided by its standard error).

SQUARED MULTIPLE CORRELATIONS FOR X - VARIABLES

VAR 1	VAR 2	VAR 3	VAR 4	VAR 5	VAR 6
0.61	0.37	0.52	0.61	0.68	0.37

SQUARED MULTIPLE CORRELATIONS FOR X - VARIABLES

VAR 7	VAR 8	VAR 9	VAR 10	VAR 11	VAR 12
0.56	0.62	0.56	0.57	0.74	0.66

SQUARED MULTIPLE CORRELATIONS FOR X - VARIABLES
VAR 13
———
(0.74)

Note: The squared multiple correlations for each variable represent the amount of variance explained by the model in each observed variable.

GOODNESS OF FIT STATISTICS

CHI-SQUARE WITH 62 DEGREES OF FREEDOM	= 211.92 (P = 0.0)
ESTIMATED NON-CENTRALITY PARAMETER (NCP)	= 149.92
MINIMUM FIT FUNCTION VALUE	= 0.98
POPULATION DISCREPANCY FUNCTION VALUE (F0)	= 0.69
ROOT MEAN SQUARE ERROR OF APPROXIMATION (RMSEA)	= 0.11
P-VALUE FOR TEST OF CLOSE FIT (RMSEA < 0.05)	= 0.00000040
EXPECTED CROSS-VALIDATION INDEX (ECVI)	= 1.25
ECVI FOR SATURATED MODEL	= 0.84
ECVI FOR INDEPENDENCE MODEL	= 8.06

```
CHI-SQUARE FOR INDEPENDENCE MODEL WITH 78 DEGREES OF
                               FREEDOM  =  1715.53
                     INDEPENDENCE AIC  =  1741.53
                            MODEL AIC  =   269.92
                        SATURATED AIC  =   182.00
                    INDEPENDENCE CAIC  =  1798.47
                           MODEL CAIC  =    96.93
                       SATURATED CAIC  =   580.57
          ROOT MEAN SQUARE RESIDUAL (RMR)  =    0.050
                      STANDARDIZED RMR  =    0.065
              GOODNESS OF FIT INDEX (GFI)  =    0.87
      ADJUSTED GOODNESS OF FIT INDEX (AGFI)  =    0.81
     PARSIMONY GOODNESS OF FIT INDEX (PGFI)  =    0.59
                   NORMED FIT INDEX (NFI)  =    0.88
               NON-NORMED FIT INDEX (NNFI)  =    0.88
          PARSIMONY NORMED FIT INDEX (PNFI)  =    0.70
              COMPARATIVE FIT INDEX (CFI)  =    0.91
             INCREMENTAL FIT INDEX (IFI)  =    0.91
               RELATIVE FIT INDEX (RFI)  =    0.84
                       CRITICAL N (CN)  =    93.55
```

Note: These are the fit indices described in Chapter 2.

```
CONFIDENCE LIMITS COULD NOT BE COMPUTED DUE TO TOO SMALL
P-VALUE FOR CHI-SQUARE
Ti Confirmatory Factor Analysis of the Union Commitment Scale
SUMMARY STATISTICS FOR FITTED RESIDUALS
SMALLEST FITTED RESIDUAL =  -0.11
MEDIAN FITTED RESIDUAL    =   0.00
LARGEST FITTED RESIDUAL   =   0.17
STEMLEAF PLOT
  - 1|1
  - 0|988766555555
  - 0|44444443333333322222222221111100000000000000000000
    0|1111122222333344444
    0|5577789
    1|33
    1|67
SUMMARY STATISTICS FOR STANDARDIZED RESIDUALS
SMALLEST STANDARDIZED RESIDUAL =  -3.71
MEDIAN STANDARDIZED RESIDUAL    =   0.00
LARGEST STANDARDIZED RESIDUAL   =   6.10
```

```
STEMLEAF PLOT
 - 3|732
 - 2|8765321
 - 1|999877666544211000
 - 0|99998876655542100000000000000000
   0|11134456889
   1|0003668899
   2|45679
   3|129
   4|27
   5|5
   6|1
```

LARGEST NEGATIVE STANDARDIZED RESIDUALS

RESIDUAL FOR	VAR 6 AND	VAR 4	-2.76
RESIDUAL FOR	VAR 10 AND	VAR 1	-2.72
RESIDUAL FOR	VAR 12 AND	VAR 3	-3.19
RESIDUAL FOR	VAR 12 AND	VAR 5	-3.28
RESIDUAL FOR	VAR 13 AND	VAR 11	-3.71

LARGEST POSITIVE STANDARDIZED RESIDUALS

RESIDUAL FOR	VAR 3 AND	VAR 1	3.19
RESIDUAL FOR	VAR 3 AND	VAR 2	2.72
RESIDUAL FOR	VAR 5 AND	VAR 4	2.88
RESIDUAL FOR	VAR 8 AND	VAR 6	4.68
RESIDUAL FOR	VAR 9 AND	VAR 6	6.10
RESIDUAL FOR	VAR 10 AND	VAR 6	5.47
RESIDUAL FOR	VAR 10 AND	VAR 9	3.90
RESIDUAL FOR	VAR 13 AND	VAR 4	3.10
RESIDUAL FOR	VAR 13 AND	VAR 7	4.24

Note: The foregoing is diagnostic information provided by LISREL. The two residual plots should look approximately normal. The listing of standardized residuals may provide clues to sources of ill-fitting models. In general, large standardized residuals indicate a lack of fit. LISREL prints any residual > 2.00.

```
Ti Confirmatory Factor Analysis of the Union Commitment Scale
MODIFICATION INDICES AND EXPECTED CHANGE
MODIFICATION INDICES FOR LAMBDA-X
```

	KSI 1	KSI 2	KSI 3
VAR 1	- -	0.47	0.49
VAR 2	- -	0.72	0.04
VAR 3	- -	0.54	6.49
VAR 4	- -	0.42	0.52

VAR 5	- -	1.38	2.01
VAR 6	- -	54.27	0.52
VAR 7	- -	1.17	4.72
VAR 8	14.95	- -	0.28
VAR 9	3.27	- -	0.04
VAR 10	4.40	- -	0.13
VAR 11	1.06	0.75	- -
VAR 12	13.77	6.52	- -
VAR 13	6.51	2.26	- -

EXPECTED CHANGE FOR LAMBDA-X

	KSI 1	KSI 2	KSI 3
VAR 1	- -	-0.06	0.06
VAR 2	- -	-0.08	-0.02
VAR 3	- -	-0.07	-0.25
VAR 4	- -	-0.05	0.06
VAR 5	- -	-0.08	-0.11
VAR 6	- -	0.54	0.06
VAR 7	- -	-0.09	0.19
VAR 8	0.38	- -	0.04
VAR 9	-0.16	- -	-0.01
VAR 10	-0.23	- -	-0.03
VAR 11	0.09	0.05	- -
VAR 12	-0.35	-0.17	- -
VAR 13	0.26	0.10	- -

STANDARDIZED EXPECTED CHANGE FOR LAMBDA-X

	KSI 1	KSI 2	KSI 3
VAR 1	- -	-0.06	0.06
VAR 2	- -	-0.08	-0.02
VAR 3	- -	-0.07	-0.25
VAR 4	- -	-0.05	0.06
VAR 5	- -	-0.08	-0.11
VAR 6	- -	0.54	0.06
VAR 7	- -	-0.09	0.19
VAR 8	0.38	- -	0.04
VAR 9	-0.16	- -	-0.01
VAR 10	-0.23	- -	-0.03
VAR 11	0.09	0.05	- -
VAR 12	-0.35	-0.17	- -
VAR 13	0.26	0.10	- -

COMPLETELY STANDARDIZED EXPECTED CHANGE FOR LAMBDA-X

	KSI 1	KSI 2	KSI 3
VAR 1	- -	-0.06	0.07
VAR 2	- -	-0.09	-0.02
VAR 3	- -	-0.07	-0.26
VAR 4	- -	-0.06	0.07
VAR 5	- -	-0.10	-0.13
VAR 6	- -	0.76	0.08
VAR 7	- -	-0.10	0.21
VAR 8	0.44	- -	0.04
VAR 9	-0.20	- -	-0.02
VAR 10	-0.23	- -	-0.03
VAR 11	0.10	0.06	- -
VAR 12	-0.36	-0.17	- -
VAR 13	0.25	0.10	- -

MODIFICATION INDICES FOR THETA-DELTA

	VAR 1	VAR 2	VAR 3	VAR 4	VAR 5	VAR 6
VAR 1	- -					
VAR 2	1.30	- -				
VAR 3	10.21	7.37	- -			
VAR 4	0.14	3.54	4.64	- -		
VAR 5	0.30	0.69	3.58	8.30	- -	
VAR 6	2.95	2.47	0.40	7.60	1.39	- -
VAR 7	0.68	2.41	3.52	1.81	0.28	0.55
VAR 8	5.47	0.27	2.28	4.90	2.01	0.01
VAR 9	0.57	0.07	0.33	0.83	4.24	20.34
VAR 10	6.27	0.01	0.05	4.73	0.58	13.32
VAR 11	0.09	8.10	0.06	4.69	0.28	4.27
VAR 12	2.94	0.77	1.24	0.27	2.77	0.03
VAR 13	0.38	5.11	2.38	10.73	0.08	2.31

MODIFICATION INDICES FOR THETA-DELTA

	VAR 7	VAR 8	VAR 9	VAR 10	VAR 11	VAR 12
VAR 7	- -					
VAR 8	0.03	- -				
VAR 9	3.40	4.46	- -			

VAR 10	0.21	3.33	15.20	- -		
VAR 11	0.86	0.59	1.61	0.00	- -	
VAR 12	1.38	1.48	0.11	0.53	6.51	- -
VAR 13	15.34	0.00	0.00	0.08	13.74	1.05

MODIFICATION INDICES FOR THETA-DELTA
VAR 13
——

- -

EXPECTED CHANGE FOR THETA-DELTA

	VAR 1	VAR 2	VAR 3	VAR 4	VAR 5	VAR 6
VAR 1	- -					
VAR 2	-0.03	- -				
VAR 3	0.10	0.09	- -			
VAR 4	0.01	-0.06	-0.07	- -		
VAR 5	-0.01	-0.02	0.05	0.07	- -	
VAR 6	-0.04	0.04	-0.02	-0.07	-0.03	- -
VAR 7	-0.02	0.05	-0.06	0.04	-0.01	-0.02
VAR 8	0.06	-0.02	-0.05	0.06	0.03	0.00
VAR 9	-0.02	-0.01	0.02	-0.02	-0.05	0.11
VAR 10	-0.08	0.00	0.01	-0.07	-0.02	0.11
VAR 11	-0.01	0.07	0.01	-0.05	0.01	0.04
VAR 12	0.05	-0.03	-0.03	-0.01	-0.04	0.00
VAR 13	-0.02	-0.07	-0.05	0.09	-0.01	-0.04

EXPECTED CHANGE FOR THETA-DELTA

	VAR 7	VAR 8	VAR 9	VAR 10	VAR 11	VAR 12
VAR 7	- -					
VAR 8	0.01	- -				
VAR 9	-0.05	-0.09	- -			
VAR 10	0.01	-0.09	0.17	- -		
VAR 11	-0.02	-0.02	0.03	0.00	- -	
VAR 12	-0.03	-0.03	-0.01	0.02	0.09	- -
VAR 13	0.11	0.00	0.00	0.01	-0.15	0.04

EXPECTED CHANGE FOR THETA-DELTA
            VAR 13
            ———

VAR 13   - -

COMPLETELY STANDARDIZED EXPECTED CHANGE FOR THETA-DELTA

	VAR 1	VAR 2	VAR 3	VAR 4	VAR 5	VAR 6
VAR 1	- -					
VAR 2	-0.04	- -				
VAR 3	0.11	0.11	- -			
VAR 4	0.01	-0.07	-0.07	- -		
VAR 5	-0.02	-0.03	0.06	0.09	- -	
VAR 6	-0.07	0.07	-0.03	-0.11	-0.04	- -
VAR 7	-0.03	0.06	-0.07	0.05	-0.02	-0.03
VAR 8	0.08	-0.02	-0.05	0.07	0.04	0.00
VAR 9	-0.03	-0.01	0.02	-0.03	-0.07	0.19
VAR 10	-0.09	0.00	0.01	-0.07	-0.02	0.15
VAR 11	-0.01	0.10	0.01	-0.06	0.01	0.07
VAR 12	0.05	-0.03	-0.04	-0.02	-0.05	0.01
VAR 13	-0.02	-0.08	-0.05	0.09	-0.01	-0.05

COMPLETELY STANDARDIZED EXPECTED CHANGE FOR THETA-DELTA

	VAR 7	VAR 8	VAR 9	VAR 10	VAR 11	VAR 12
VAR 7	- -					
VAR 8	0.01	- -				
VAR 9	-0.07	-0.12	- -			
VAR 10	0.02	-0.10	0.21	- -		
VAR 11	-0.03	-0.02	0.04	0.00	- -	
VAR 12	-0.04	-0.04	-0.01	0.02	0.10	- -
VAR 13	0.12	0.00	0.00	0.01	-0.16	0.04

COMPLETELY STANDARDIZED EXPECTED CHANGE FOR THETA-DELTA
            VAR 13
            ———

VAR 13   - -

MAXIMUM MODIFICATION INDEX IS   54.27 FOR ELEMENT (6, 2) OF LAMBDA-X

Note: For each fixed parameter, LISREL reports the modification index and the expected amount of change. The modification index is the amount by which the model χ^2 will decrease if the parameter is freed.

The expected change for the parameter is the expected value of the parameter if it were freed. The standardized and completed standardized expected changes are the expected values in the standardized and completely standardized solution if the parameter were freed.

Ti Confirmatory Factor Analysis of the Union Commitment
Scale

STANDARDIZED SOLUTION

LAMBDA-X

	KSI 1	KSI 2	KSI 3
VAR 1	0.73	- -	- -
VAR 2	0.52	- -	- -
VAR 3	0.71	- -	- -
VAR 4	0.72	- -	- -
VAR 5	0.70	- -	- -
VAR 6	0.43	- -	- -
VAR 7	0.68	- -	- -
VAR 8	- -	0.69	- -
VAR 9	- -	0.63	- -
VAR 10	- -	0.75	- -
VAR 11	- -	- -	0.73
VAR 12	- -	- -	0.80
VAR 13	- -	- -	0.90

PHI

	KSI 1	KSI 2	KSI 3
KSI 1	1.00		
KSI 2	0.72	1.00	
KSI 3	0.78	0.56	1.00

Note: The standardized solution is based on standardized latent variables but unstandardized observed variables. As a result, the parameters are not constrained to have an absolute value less than 1.

Ti Confirmatory Factor Analysis of the Union Commitment Scale
COMPLETELY STANDARDIZED SOLUTION
LAMBDA-X

	KSI 1	KSI 2	KSI 3
VAR 1	0.78	- -	- -
VAR 2	0.61	- -	- -
VAR 3	0.72	- -	- -
VAR 4	0.78	- -	- -
VAR 5	0.82	- -	- -
VAR 6	0.61	- -	- -
VAR 7	0.75	- -	- -
VAR 8	- -	0.79	- -
VAR 9	- -	0.75	- -
VAR 10	- -	0.75	- -
VAR 11	- -	- -	0.86
VAR 12	- -	- -	0.82
VAR 13	- -	- -	0.86

PHI

	KSI 1	KSI 2	KSI 3
KSI 1	1.00		
KSI 2	0.72	1.00	
KSI 3	0.78	0.56	1.00

THETA-DELTA

VAR 1	VAR 2	VAR 3	VAR 4	VAR 5	VAR 6
0.39	0.63	0.48	0.39	0.32	0.63

THETA-DELTA

VAR 7	VAR 8	VAR 9	VAR 10	VAR 11	VAR12
0.44	0.38	0.44	0.43	0.26	0.34

THETA-DELTA

VAR 13
0.26

Note: The completely standardized solution is based on standardized latent and observed variables. These are the values that typically are reported in a results section.

TABLE 5.1 Fit Indices for the Models

Model	χ^2	df	GFI	AGFI	RMSEA	NFI	CFI	PNFI	PGFI
1. 3-factor oblique	211.92	62	.87	.81	.11	.88	.91	.70	.59
2. 3-factor orthogonal	449.50	65	.78	.70	.17	.74	.77	.61	.56
3. 2-factor oblique	359.39	64	.77	.67	.15	.79	.82	.65	.54
4. 1-factor	414.10	65	.74	.64	.16	.76	.79	.63	.64

Assessment of Fit

Given the models described earlier, assessing the fit of the three-factor model is based on (a) whether the model fits better than rival specifications and (b) whether the model provides a good absolute fit to the data. The fit indices for all the models described earlier are presented in Table 5.1.

As shown, the fit indices all converge in suggesting the superiority of the model hypothesizing three oblique factors. Comparison with the other models shows that the three-factor (oblique) model provides a better fit to the data than does a model hypothesizing three orthogonal factors [$\chi^2_{\text{difference}}(3) = 237.58, p < .01$], two oblique factors [$\chi^2_{\text{difference}}(2) = 147.47, p < .01$], or one factor [$\chi^2_{\text{difference}}(3) = 202.18, p < .01$]. Moreover, inspection of the indices of parsimonious fit (i.e., the PNFI and PGFI) suggest that the three-factor model provides the most parsimonious fit to the data.

As is typical in confirmatory factor analysis (Kelloway, 1995, 1996), although the three-factor model provides a better fit to the data than do rival specifications, the model itself does not provide a very good fit to the data. Although inspection of the preceding printout suggests that all the estimated parameters in the hypothesized three-factor model are significant, the χ^2 associated with the model is also significant. With the exception of the CFI (CFI = .91), all the fit indices are outside the bounds that indicate a good fit to the data (e.g., GFI, AGFI, NFI < .90; RMSEA > .10). Thus, the most that can be concluded from these results is that the hypothesized three-factor model provides a better fit than do plausible rival specifications.

Model Modification

Faced with results like these, researchers may well be tempted to engage in a post hoc specification search to improve the fit of the model. Given that all the estimated parameters are significant, theory trimming (i.e., deleting nonsignificant paths) does not seem to be a viable option. Theory building (i.e., adding parameters based on the empirical results) remains an option.

Inspection of the LISREL-produced modification indices suggests several likely additional parameters (i.e., modification indices greater than 5.0). Most strikingly, the largest modification index (54.27) suggests freeing the path from the second factor to the sixth item. Although the modification index suggests that a substantial improvement in fit could be obtained from making this modification, the reader is reminded of the dangers associated with post hoc model modifications. In this case, I would not typically make the change because (a) of the dangers of empirically generated modifications, (b) there is no theoretical justification for the change, and (c) the item is clearly not designed to assess Willingness to Work for the Union.

Sample Results Section

We conclude this example of confirmatory factor analysis with the presentation of a sample results section. A useful guide to reporting the results of structural equation modeling was provided by Raykov, Tomer, and Nesselroade (1991). As a minimum set of reporting standards, they suggest that all reports of structural equation modeling analyses include

1. a graphic presentation of the structural equation model following conventional symbols (see, for example, Bentler, 1990; Jöreskog & Sörbom, 1992);

2. parameters for the structural equation run, including the type of matrix analyzed, the treatment of missing values and outliers, the number of groups to be analyzed (if appropriate), and the method of parameter estimation;

3. an assessment of model fit, such as Condition 10 tests (James et al., 1982). As previously noted, researchers are well advised to report multiple fit indices and should report indices that reflect different conceptions of model fit;

4. an examination of the obtained solution including the Condition 9 tests (James et al., 1982) referred to earlier, the coefficient of determination, the R^2 values associated with each equation in the model, and examination of direct/indirect effects (when appropriate);

5. nested model comparisons; and

6. model modifications and alternate models—When the model is modified on the basis of empirical results, a minimum standard of reporting would include the change in overall fit associated with modification as well as the change in specific parameters as a result of model modification. As noted earlier, such modifications should be treated as exploratory until cross-validated on an independent sample.

Results

All model tests were based on the covariance matrix and used maximum likelihood estimation as implemented in LISREL VIII (Jöreskog & Sörbom, 1992).

Fit indices for the four models are presented in Table 5.1. As shown, the indices converge in suggesting the superiority of the model hypothesizing three oblique factors. In particular, the three-factor (oblique) model provides a better fit to the data than does a model hypothesizing three orthogonal factors [$\chi^2_{\text{difference}}(3) = 237.58, p < .01$], two oblique

TABLE 5.2 Standardized Parameter Estimates for the Three-Factor Model

Item	Union Loyalty	Willingness to Work	Responsibility to the Union	R^2
1	0.78			0.61
2	0.61			0.37
3	0.72			0.52
4	0.78			0.61
5	0.82			0.68
6	0.61			0.37
7	0.75			0.56
8		0.79		0.62
9		0.75		0.56
10		0.75		0.57
11			0.86	0.74
12			0.82	0.66
13			0.86	0.74

TABLE 5.3 Interfactor Correlations

	1	2	3
1. Union Loyalty	1.00		
2. Willingness to Work for the Union	0.72	1.00	
3. Responsibility to the Union	0.78	0.56	1.00

NOTE: All parameters $p < .01$.

factors [$\chi^2_{\text{difference}}(2) = 147.47, p < .01$], or one factor [$\chi^2_{\text{difference}}(3) = 202.18, p < .01$]. Moreover, inspection of the indices of parsimonious fit (i.e., the PNFI and PGFI) suggests that the three-factor model provides the most parsimonious fit to the data.

Standardized parameter estimates for the model are presented in Table 5.2. As shown, model parameters were all significant ($p < .01$) and explained substantial amounts of item variance (R^2 ranged from 0.37 to 0.74). As shown in Table 5.3, the three factors were significantly correlated ($r = .56, .72,$ and $.78$).

CHAPTER 6 *Observed Variable*
Path Analysis

Path analysis with observed variables is the "oldest" variety of structural equation modeling. In contrast to the assessment of a measurement model as presented in the previous chapter, the goal of path analysis is to test a "structural" model, that is, a model comprising theoretically based statements of relationships among constructs.

For an example of path analysis, I will use a scaled-down version of the model presented by Kelloway and Barling (1993). The intent of the research was to predict union members' involvement in union activities (attending meetings, serving as officers, reading union literature, voting in elections). The theoretical development of the model relied heavily on Fishbein and Ajzen's (1975) theory of reasoned action. In brief, the theory of reasoned action suggests that the best predictor of actual behavior is an individual's intent to engage in the behavior. In turn, behavioral intentions are predicted by one's attitudes toward the activity and subjective norms. One's beliefs about the activity predict attitudes toward the behavior.

Model Specification

In our study, we had measures of participation in union activities (the behavior), willingness to participate in the union (which we treated as a behavioral intention), union loyalty (attitudes toward the union), and subjective norms (perceptions of family, friends, and important people

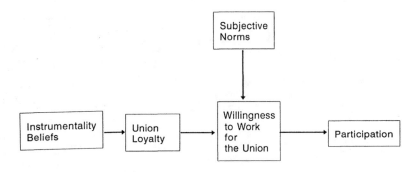

Figure 6.1.

regarding participation). Finally, we constructed a scale assessing individuals' beliefs regarding the instrumentality of participation. The path diagram corresponding to our translation of Fishbein and Ajzen's (1975) theory is shown in Figure 6.1.

Note that in this model we have two exogenous variables (norms and instrumentality) that are allowed to correlate freely. There are three endogenous variables (loyalty, willingness, and actual participation). Attitudes are predicted by instrumentality beliefs. Willingness to work for the union is hypothesized to be totally a function of attitudes and norms. Participation is hypothesized to be predicted by willingness.

Because this is a path analysis using only manifest or observed variables, the LISREL model focuses only on the structural model (matrices **BE**, **GA**, and **PS**). The measurement model is ignored. Note that one of the assumptions of observed variable path analysis is that all variables are measured without error. Although this assumption is untenable in the social sciences, it typically is satisfied by the requirement that all variables manifest high levels of reliability (often defined as alphas > .70; Pedhazur, 1982). This assumption was met in the current example (Kelloway & Barling, 1993).

From Pictures to LISREL

The LISREL matrices corresponding to the path diagram are presented below. As a reminder, in making the translation from path diagrams to LISREL matrices, remember that columns cause rows.

```
BETA (relates endogenous to endogenous)
                 Particip        Willingn          Loyalty
                 ‾‾‾‾‾           ‾‾‾‾‾             ‾‾‾‾‾

Participation    FIxed           FRee              FIxed
Willingness      FIxed           FIxed             FRee
Loyalty          FIxed           FIxed             FIxed

GAMMA (relates exogenous to endogenous)
                 Instrume        Norms
                 ‾‾‾‾‾           ‾‾‾‾‾

Participation    FIxed           FIxed
Willingness      FIxed           FRee
Loyalty          FRee            FIxed

PSI (residual variances of endogenous)
Participation    Willingn        Loyalty
                 ‾‾‾‾‾           ‾‾‾‾‾

Free             FRee            Free
```

The PSI matrix in this model deserves some comment. PSI contains the residuals of the endogenous variables. Residual variances are represented on the diagonal, with correlated errors of prediction (correlated residuals) in the off-diagonal elements. One of the assumptions of traditional path analysis is that the model contains all relevant causal influences for the endogenous variables (the model is fully specified). Under this assumption, the covariances of the endogenous variables are fully explained by the posited relationships in the model; hence, there are no correlated errors of prediction.

In the current example, I explicitly tell LISREL that there are no covariances or correlations between the endogenous variables (after accounting for the structural relations). Operationally, this means that PSI is a diagonal matrix (a vector containing only the residual variances of the endogenous variables).

Alternative Models

For our purposes, a reasonable alternative to the proposed model is based on the findings of Fullagar and colleagues (1992) and Kelloway and Barling (1993). In both studies, the authors reported that in addition to the paths presented in the Fishbein and Ajzen-based model, subjective norms was a predictor of union loyalty. Adding this path to the proposed model creates a plausible alternative model that stands in nested sequence with the original model.

When the literature does not offer a plausible rival model specification, alternative models can be generated by considering (a) omitted parameters and (b) indirect effects in structural equation models. I have previously noted (Kelloway, 1996) that most researchers build models from the "bottom up," offering a theoretic or empirical rationale for the inclusion of certain parameters in their models.

In contrast to this procedure, I also have suggested (Kelloway, 1995) that there is some advantage in developing models from the top down, that is, providing justification for the omission of parameters from the model. The rationale for this suggestion is that tests of model fit are, in essence, tests of omitted parameters (Brannick, 1995; Kelloway, 1995). That is, because the just-identified or saturated model always provides a perfect fit to the data, testing an overidentified model for fit is, in essence, testing whether the overidentifying restrictions (e.g., omitted paths) are necessary.

Thus, although researchers should continue to justify the inclusion of specific parameters in their model, I suggest that there is considerable merit in paying equal attention to the parameters omitted from the model. When researchers have no particular justification for the inclusion or omission of a particular parameter, an opportunity is created to formulate and test competing models.

In particular, researchers need to consider the implications of indirect relationships posited in their models. The indirect relationship of X on Z (through Y) can be diagrammed as $X \rightarrow Y \rightarrow Z$. There are at least two interpretations of such relationships. First, Y may be viewed as a mediator of the $X \rightarrow Z$ relationship such that the effects of X on Z are completely mediated by Y. The rationale and sequence for mediator tests is presented by Baron and Kenny (1986). The first condition of such a test is that X and Z are significantly related. In many applications of structural models containing an indirect relationship, however, there is no significant relationship between X and Z, and the indirect relationship may be more appropriately thought of as one of sequential causation. Considering the interpretation of indirect relationships a priori would assist in the identification of alternative models for analyses (Kelloway, 1995) and assist researchers in formulating more precise hypotheses in their models.

In the current example, there are several mediated relationships posited: Willingness to work for the union mediates the relationship

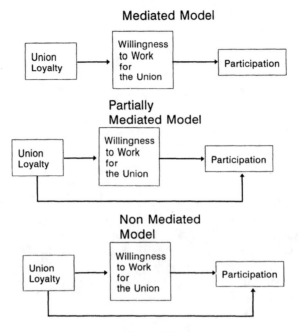

Figure 6.2.

between loyalty and participation as well as the link between subjective norms and participation. Similarly, loyalty mediates the relationship between instrumentality beliefs and willingness. Each of these mediational relationships provides an opportunity to generate plausible rival specifications within a nesting sequence.

For each mediated relationship in a model, there are two plausible rival specifications: a partially mediated model and a nonmediated model. To illustrate these models, consider the diagrams presented in Figure 6.2. Each diagram gives a plausible account of how loyalty is related to participation. First, the mediated model suggests that loyalty causes willingness, which in turn causes participation. Second, the partially mediated model suggests that loyalty causes both willingness and participation directly. In the partially mediated model, willingness also is hypothesized as a cause of participation. Finally, the nonmediated model suggests that loyalty causes both willingness and participation but there is no direct relationship between willingness and participation.

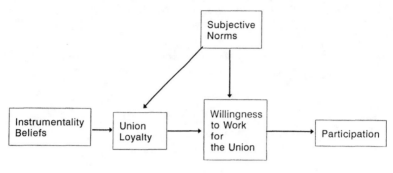

Figure 6.3.

As was the case for confirmatory path analysis, another source of alternative models is the research literature. With reference to the current example, Fullagar and colleagues (1992) found that subjective norms were a predictor of union loyalty as well as willingness to work for the union. Adding this path to the original model gives the model depicted in Figure 6.3.

Identification

Bollen (1989) cites four rules for the identification of structural models: the t rule (see Chapter 5), the null B rule, the recursive rule, and rank and order conditions.[1] The null B rule states that a model is identified if there are no predictive relationships between the endogenous variables (in LISREL terminology, leading to the definition of the beta matrix as a null matrix). The null B rule is a sufficient condition for model identification, and its most common example is the estimation of a multiple regression equation. Note that the null B rule is a sufficient but not necessary condition for the identification of a structural model.

The recursive rule states that recursive models, incorporating only one-way causal flow, are identified; again, recursion is a sufficient condition for identification of structural models. Again, recursion is a sufficient but not necessary condition for identification. Although we shall not deal with nonrecursive models, it is possible to estimate identified models allowing for bidirectional causality. Given our focus on recursive models, the models described earlier are, by definition, identified.

Estimation

The code used to estimate the model is given below, with explanatory comments. Following the code, the annotated output from the LISREL job is presented, followed by an edited output from a second run incorporating the effect of subjective norms on loyalty.

```
TI Reasoned action model of union participation
DA NI = 5 NO = 202 MA = CM
```

Note: There are five input variables, based on 202 observations, and I want LISREL to analyze the covariance matrix.

```
CM SY
  2.637
  3.071   15.972
  3.550   16.014   31.921
  2.615   10.719   19.247   31.002
  5.495   24.191   33.299   25.070   132.315
```

Note: This time I am reading in a lower diagonal covariance matrix (variances on the diagonal, covariances on the off-diagonal).

```
LA
  'Participation' 'Willingness' 'Loyalty'
  'Instrumentality' 'Sub. Norms'
```

Note: These are the variable labels.

```
MO NX = 2 NY = 3 PS = DI,FR BE = FU,FI GA = FU,FI
```

Note: I have specified that there are two exogenous (NX) and three endogenous (NY) variables. I have declared PSI to be a diagonal matrix (no off-diagonal elements) that is freely estimated. This tells LISREL to estimate the residual variances (but not covariances) for the endogenous variables. As a matter of habit, I always declare that both GAmma and BEta are full (rectangular) and fixed. This procedure allows me to ensure that the only elements to be estimated in this model are the ones I explicitly tell LISREL to free.

```
FR BE(1,2) BE(2,3)
```

Note: This code tells LISREL to estimate the path from willingness (2) to participation (1) and the path from loyalty (3) to willingness (2).

```
FR GA(3,1) GA(2,2)
```

Note: This code tells LISREL to estimate the paths from both exogenous variables, beliefs (1) and norms (2), to loyalty (3) and willingness (2).

```
OU ML TO MI SS TV EF
```

Note: This code specifies that I want maximum likelihood estimation (ML), with the printout to be 80 columns wide (TO). I also have specified that I would like to see the modification indices (MI), the standardized solution (SS), the t values for parameters (TV), and the estimates for all effects (both direct and indirect) in the model (EF).

```
ANNOTATED OUTPUT
NUMBER OF INPUT VARIABLES 5
NUMBER OF Y - VARIABLES   3
NUMBER OF X - VARIABLES   2
NUMBER OF ETA - VARIABLES 3
NUMBER OF KSI - VARIABLES 2
NUMBER OF OBSERVATIONS  202
```

TI REASONED ACTION MODEL OF UNION PARTICIPATION
COVARIANCE MATRIX TO BE ANALYZED

	Particip	Willingn	Loyalty	Instrume	Subjecti
Particip	2.64				
Willingn	3.07	15.97			
Loyalty	3.55	16.01	31.92		
Instrume	2.62	10.72	19.25	31.00	
Subjecti	5.50	24.19	33.30	25.07	132.32

TI REASONED ACTION MODEL OF UNION PARTICIPATION PARAMETER
SPECIFICATIONS
BETA

	Particip	Willingn	Loyalty
Particip	0	1	0
Willingn	0	0	2
Loyalty	0	0	0

GAMMA

	Instrume	Subjecti
Particip	0	0
Willingn	0	3
Loyalty	4	0

PHI

	Instrume	Subjecti
Instrume	5	
Subjecti	6	7

PSI

Particip	Willingn	Loyalty
8	9	10

Note: Once again, the LISREL output begins by repeating the model specification. This information always should be scanned to ensure that the model you think you are testing is the one that the program actually is working with.

```
TI REASONED ACTION MODEL OF UNION PARTICIPATION
Number of Iterations = 6
LISREL ESTIMATES (MAXIMUM LIKELIHOOD)
BETA
```

	Particip	Willingn	Loyalty
Particip	- -	0.19	- -
		(0.03)	
		7.30	
Willingn	- -	- -	0.42
			(0.04)
			12.02
Loyalty	- -	- -	- -

GAMMA

	Instrume	Subjecti
Particip	- -	- -
Willingn	- -	0.08
		(0.02)
		4.45
Loyalty	0.62	- -
	(0.06)	
	10.91	

Note: These are the maximum likelihood estimates of the parameters, followed by the standard errors (in parentheses) and the t values (parameter/standard error). In regression terms, these are the unstandardized regression weights.

COVARIANCE MATRIX OF Y AND X

	Particip	Willingn	Loyalty	Instrume	Subjecti
Particip	2.59				
Willingn	2.85	14.82			
Loyalty	2.82	14.65	31.92		
Instrume	1.93	10.04	19.25	31.00	
Subjecti	3.21	16.71	15.56	25.07	132.32

PHI

	Instrume	Subjecti
Instrume	31.00	
Subjecti	25.07	132.32

PSI

Particip	Willingn	Loyalty
2.05	7.36	19.97
(0.21)	(0.74)	(2.00)
9.97	9.97	9.97

SQUARED MULTIPLE CORRELATIONS FOR STRUCTURAL EQUATIONS

Particip	Willingn	Loyalty
0.21	.50	0.37

Note: For each endogenous variable in the model, LISREL calculates the R^2 value, which is interpreted exactly the same as R^2 values in regression. In the current case, the model is able to explain 21% of the variance in participation, 50% of the variance in willingness to work for the union, and 37% of the variance in union loyalty.

```
GOODNESS OF FIT STATISTICS
           CHI-SQUARE WITH 5 DEGREES OF FREEDOM =  33.24 (P = 0.0000034)
        ESTIMATED NON-CENTRALITY PARAMETER (NCP) =  28.24
                    MINIMUM FIT FUNCTION VALUE =   0.17
        POPULATION DISCREPANCY FUNCTION VALUE (F0) =   0.14
           ROOT MEAN SQUARE ERROR OF APPROXIMATION
                                       (RMSEA) =   0.17
     P-VALUE FOR TEST OF CLOSE FIT (RMSEA < 0.05) =   0.00018
          EXPECTED CROSS-VALIDATION INDEX (ECVI) =   0.27
                   ECVI FOR SATURATED MODEL =   0.15
                ECVI FOR INDEPENDENCE MODEL =   1.90
   CHI-SQUARE FOR INDEPENDENCE MODEL WITH 10
                       DEGREES OF FREEDOM = 367.51
                      INDEPENDENCE AIC = 377.51
                            MODEL AIC =  53.24
                        SATURATED AIC =  30.00
                  INDEPENDENCE CAIC = 399.05
                          MODEL CAIC =  96.33
                      SATURATED CAIC =  94.62
          ROOT MEAN SQUARE RESIDUAL (RMR) =   5.04
                      STANDARDIZED RMR =   0.098
            GOODNESS OF FIT INDEX (GFI) =   0.94
   ADJUSTED GOODNESS OF FIT INDEX (AGFI) =   0.83
  PARSIMONY GOODNESS OF FIT INDEX (PGFI) =   0.31
                   NORMED FIT INDEX (NFI) =   0.91
               NON-NORMED FIT INDEX (NNFI) =   0.84
          PARSIMONY NORMED FIT INDEX (PNFI) =   0.45
            COMPARATIVE FIT INDEX (CFI) =   0.92
            INCREMENTAL FIT INDEX (IFI) =   0.92
               RELATIVE FIT INDEX (RFI) =   0.82
                        CRITICAL N (CN) =  92.23
```

Note: Again, these are the fit indices described in Chapter 2. Note that the model falls in the awkward category of a "reasonable but not outstanding" fit to the data. That is, the NFI, GFI, CFI, and IFI all indicate an acceptable fit to the data; however, the χ^2, RMSEA, standardized RMR, AGFI, and RFI and NNFI all indicate that the model is not a good fit to the data.

```
CONFIDENCE LIMITS COULD NOT BE COMPUTED DUE TO TOO SMALL
P-VALUE FOR CHI-SQUARE
TI REASONED ACTION MODEL OF UNION PARTICIPATION SUMMARY
STATISTICS FOR FITTED RESIDUALS
SMALLEST FITTED RESIDUAL =    0.00
MEDIAN FITTED RESIDUAL    =    0.68
LARGEST FITTED RESIDUAL   =   17.73
STEMLEAF PLOT
  0|0000000111112
  0|7
  1|
  1|8
SUMMARY STATISTICS FOR STANDARDIZED RESIDUALS
SMALLEST STANDARDIZED RESIDUAL =    0.00
MEDIAN STANDARDIZED RESIDUAL    =    1.65
LARGEST STANDARDIZED RESIDUAL   =    3.93
STEMLEAF PLOT
  0|000005
  1|2699
  2|666
  3|19
LARGEST POSITIVE STANDARDIZED RESIDUALS
RESIDUAL FOR Subjecti AND Willingn   3.05
RESIDUAL FOR Subjecti AND  Loyalty   3.93
TI REASONED ACTION MODEL OF UNION PARTICIPATION
MODIFICATION INDICES AND EXPECTED CHANGE

MODIFICATION INDICES FOR BETA
               Particip   Willingn  Loyalty
               ____       ____      ____

Particip       - -        - -       1.25
Willingn       1.84       - -       - -
Loyalty        0.57       2.83      - -
```

EXPECTED CHANGE FOR BETA

	Particip	Willingn	Loyalty
Particip	- -	- -	0.03
Willingn	-0.26	- -	- -
Loyalty	0.18	0.30	- -

STANDARDIZED EXPECTED CHANGE FOR BETA

	Particip	Willingn	Loyalty
Particip	- -	- -	0.00
Willingn	-0.04	- -	- -
Loyalty	0.02	0.01	- -

MODIFICATION INDICES FOR GAMMA

	Instrume	Subjecti
Particip	1.25	0.62
Willingn	0.72	- -
Loyalty	- -	28.25

EXPECTED CHANGE FOR GAMMA

	Instrume	Subjecti
Particip	0.02	0.01
Willingn	0.04	- -
Loyalty	- -	0.16

STANDARDIZED EXPECTED CHANGE FOR GAMMA

	Instrume	Subjecti
Particip	0.08	0.05
Willingn	0.06	- -
Loyalty	- -	0.32

MODIFICATION INDICES FOR PSI

	Particip	Willingn	Loyalty
Particip	- -		
Willingn	1.84	- -	
Loyalty	0.10	0.72	- -

```
EXPECTED CHANGE FOR PSI
                  Particip   Willingn   Loyalty
                  _____     _____     _____

Particip           - -
Willingn          -0.52       - -
Loyalty            0.17      -1.26        - -

STANDARDIZED EXPECTED CHANGE FOR PSI
                  Particip   Willingn   Loyalty
                  _____     _____     _____

Particip           - -
Willingn          -0.08       - -
Loyalty            0.02      -0.06        - -
MAXIMUM MODIFICATION INDEX IS 28.25 FOR ELEMENT (3, 2) OF
GAMMA
```

Note: The residuals, modification indices, expected changes, and standardized expected changes provide information about the sources of the model's lack of fit. They converge in suggesting that the fit of the model would be improved substantially by allowing a path between subjective norms and union loyalty, Gamma (3, 2).

```
TI REASONED ACTION MODEL OF UNION PARTICIPATION
STANDARDIZED SOLUTION
BETA
                  Particip   Willingn   Loyalty
                  _____     _____     _____

Particip           - -        0.46       - -
Willingn           - -        - -        0.62
Loyalty            - -        - -        - -

GAMMA
                  Instrume   Subjecti
                  _____     _____

Particip           - -        - -
Willingn           - -        0.23
Loyalty           0.61        - -
```

Note: These are the standardized parameter estimates (in regression terms, the βs). These are the values that typically would be reported in a results section.

```
CORRELATION MATRIX OF Y AND X
            Particip  Willingn   Loyalty Instrume   Subjecti
            ‗‗‗‗      ‗‗‗‗       ‗‗‗‗     ‗‗‗‗       ‗‗‗‗

Particip    1.00
Willingn    0.46      1.00
Loyalty     0.31      0.67       1.00
Instrume    0.22      0.47       0.61     1.00
Subjecti    0.17      0.38       0.24     0.39       1.00


PSI
            Particip  Willingn   Loyalty
            ‗‗‗‗      ‗‗‗‗       ‗‗‗‗

            0.79      0.50       0.63


        REGRESSION MATRIX Y ON X (STANDARDIZED)
            Instrume  Subjecti
            ‗‗‗‗      ‗‗‗‗

Particip    0.17      0.11
Willingn    0.38      0.23
Loyalty     0.61      - -
```

Note: LISREL reports the regression equation for each endogenous (Y) variable predicted by each exogenous (X) variable.

```
TI REASONED ACTION MODEL OF UNION PARTICIPATION TOTAL AND
INDIRECT EFFECTS
TOTAL EFFECTS OF X ON Y
            Instrume  Subjecti
            ‗‗‗‗      ‗‗‗‗

Particip    0.05      0.01
           (0.01)    (0.00)
            5.42      3.80
Willingn    0.26      0.08
           (0.03)    (0.02)
            8.08      4.45
Loyalty     0.62      - -
           (0.06)
           10.91
```

Note: The total effect of an exogenous variable on an endogenous variable is the sum of the direct (simple paths) and indirect (compound paths) linking the two variables. LISREL reports the total effects, followed by the standard error of the effects and a significance test of the total effect (effect/standard error).

```
INDIRECT EFFECTS OF X ON Y
                   Instrume Subjecti
                   ————     ————

Particip           0.05     0.01
                  (0.01)   (0.00)
                   5.42     3.80

Willingn           0.26      - -
                  (0.03)
                   8.08

Loyalty            - -       - -
```

Note: LISREL then decomposes the total effect and presents separate information on the indirect effects. (Recall that the direct effects are the parameters estimated in the model; therefore, they have been presented previously.)

```
TOTAL EFFECTS OF Y ON Y
                   Particip Willingn  Loyalty
                   ————     ————      ————

Particip           - -      0.19      0.08
                           (0.03)    (0.01)
                            7.30      6.24

Willingn           - -      - -       0.42
                                     (0.04)
                                     12.02

Loyalty            - -      - -       - -
```

Note: This is the same information as presented above (total effect, standard errors, and significance test). This time the effects under consideration are the effects of the endogenous (Y) variables on other endogenous (Y) variables.

LARGEST EIGENVALUE OF B*B' (STABILITY INDEX) IS 0.178

Note: The stability index is rarely reported and is most useful when estimating nonrecursive models.

INDIRECT EFFECTS OF Y ON Y

	Particip	Willingn	Loyalty
Particip	- -	- -	0.08
			(0.01)
			6.24
Willingn	- -	- -	- -
Loyalty	- -	- -	- -

Note: Again, the indirect effects of the endogenous variables on the endogenous variables are presented. In the model, there is only one compound path linking endogenous variables (from loyalty to willingness to participation). Thus, only the indirect effect of loyalty on participation is reported.

TI REASONED ACTION MODEL OF UNION PARTICIPATION
STANDARDIZED TOTAL AND INDIRECT EFFECTS
STANDARDIZED TOTAL EFFECTS OF X ON Y

	Instrume	Subjecti
Particip	0.17	0.11
Willingn	0.38	0.23
Loyalty	0.61	- -

STANDARDIZED INDIRECT EFFECTS OF X ON Y

	Instrume	Subjecti
Particip	0.17	0.11
Willingn	0.38	- -
Loyalty	- -	- -

STANDARDIZED TOTAL EFFECTS OF Y ON Y

	Particip	Willingn	Loyalty
Particip	- -	0.46	0.28
Willingn	- -	- -	0.62
Loyalty	- -	- -	- -

```
STANDARDIZED INDIRECT EFFECTS OF Y ON Y
               Particip Willingn  Loyalty
               _____  _____  _____

Particip        - -      - -      0.28
Willingn        - -      - -      - -
Loyalty         - -      - -      - -
```

Note: The same information about effects reported in standardized form. The standardized estimates allow the direct comparison of effect sizes.

```
Second Run (Adding subjective norms - loyalty)
TI      REASONED ACTION MODEL OF UNION PARTICIPATION
DA      NI = 5 NO = 202 MA = CM
CM      SY
  2.637
  3.071   15.972
  3.550   16.014   31.921
  2.615   10.719   19.247   31.002
  5.495   24.191   33.299   25.070   132.315
LA
'Participation' 'Willingness' 'Loyalty'·
'Instrumentality' 'Subjective Norms'
MO NX = 2 NY = 3 BE = FU,FI GA = FU,FI PS = DI,FR
FR BE(1,2) BE(2,3)
FR GA(3,1) GA(2,2) GA(3,2)
```

Note: I have now added the path from subjective norms to loyalty, GA(3, 2).

```
OU ML SC TV EF
TI REASONED ACTION MODEL OF UNION PARTICIPATION
Number of Iterations = 5
LISREL ESTIMATES (MAXIMUM LIKELIHOOD)
BETA
               Particip Willingn  Loyalty
               _____  _____  _____

Particip        - -      0.19      - -
                        (0.03)
                         7.58
```

Willingn	- -	- -	0.42
			(0.04)
			10.63
Loyalty	- -	- -	- -

GAMMA

	Instrume	Subjecti
Particip	- -	- -
Willingn	- -	0.08
		(0.02)
		3.94
Loyalty	0.49	0.16
	(0.06)	(0.03)
	8.60	5.70

Note: All parameters are significant.

SQUARED MULTIPLE CORRELATIONS FOR STRUCTURAL EQUATIONS

Particip	Willingn	Loyalty
0.22	0.54	0.46

GOODNESS OF FIT STATISTICS

CHI-SQUARE WITH 4 DEGREES OF FREEDOM = 2.80 (P = 0.59)
ESTIMATED NON-CENTRALITY PARAMETER (NCP) = 0.0
90 PERCENT CONFIDENCE INTERVAL FOR NCP = (0.0 ; 6.59)
MINIMUM FIT FUNCTION VALUE = 0.014
POPULATION DISCREPANCY FUNCTION VALUE (F0) = 0.0
90 PERCENT CONFIDENCE INTERVAL FOR F0 = (0.0 ; 0.033)
ROOT MEAN SQUARE ERROR OF APPROXIMATION (RMSEA) = 0.0
90 PERCENT CONFIDENCE INTERVAL FOR RMSEA = (0.0 ; 0.091)
P-VALUE FOR TEST OF CLOSE FIT (RMSEA < 0.05) = 0.78
EXPECTED CROSS-VALIDATION INDEX (ECVI) = 0.12
90 PERCENT CONFIDENCE INTERVAL FOR ECVI = (0.13 ; 0.16)
ECVI FOR SATURATED MODEL = 0.15
ECVI FOR INDEPENDENCE MODEL = 1.90
CHI-SQUARE FOR INDEPENDENCE MODEL WITH 10
DEGREES OF FREEDOM = 367.51
INDEPENDENCE AIC = 377.51
MODEL AIC = 24.80
SATURATED AIC = 30.00
INDEPENDENCE CAIC = 399.05
MODEL CAIC = 72.19
SATURATED CAIC = 94.62

```
        ROOT MEAN SQUARE RESIDUAL (RMR) =    0.35
                       STANDARDIZED RMR  =    0.028
              GOODNESS OF FIT INDEX (GFI) =    0.99
     ADJUSTED GOODNESS OF FIT INDEX (AGFI) =    0.98
   PARSIMONY GOODNESS OF FIT INDEX (PGFI) =    0.27
                  NORMED FIT INDEX (NFI) =    0.99
              NON-NORMED FIT INDEX (NNFI) =    1.01
       PARSIMONY NORMED FIT INDEX (PNFI) =    0.40
            COMPARATIVE FIT INDEX (CFI) =    1.00
            INCREMENTAL FIT INDEX (IFI) =    1.00
               RELATIVE FIT INDEX (RFI) =    0.98
                         CRITICAL N (CN) = 954.97
```

Note: The model now provides an acceptable fit to the data.

```
MODIFICATION INDICES FOR BETA
                Particip  Willingn   Loyalty
                 _____    _____    _____

Particip         - -       - -       1.37
Willingn         1.72      - -       - -
Loyalty          - -       0.66      - -

MODIFICATION INDICES FOR GAMMA
                Instrume  Subjecti
                 _____    _____

Particip         1.22      0.73
Willingn         0.66      - -
Loyalty          - -       - -

MODIFICATION INDICES FOR PSI
                Particip  Willingn   Loyalty
                 _____    _____    _____

Particip         - -
Willingn         1.72      - -
Loyalty          0.03      0.66      - -
MAXIMUM MODIFICATION INDEX IS 1.72 FOR ELEMENT (2, 1) OF
BETA
```

Note: The modification indices suggest no further changes to the model.

```
TI REASONED ACTION MODEL OF UNION PARTICIPATION
STANDARDIZED SOLUTION
BETA
            Particip  Willingn  Loyalty
            _____  _____  _____

Particip     - -       0.47      - -
Willingn     - -       - -       0.60
Loyalty      - -       - -       - -

GAMMA
            Instrume  Subjecti
            _____  _____

Particip     - -       - -
Willingn     - -       0.22
Loyalty      0.49      0.32
```

Fit and Model Modification

The original model provided only a modest fit to the data. Adding the path from subjective norms to union loyalty substantially improved the fit of the model, $\chi^2_{\text{difference}}(1) = 30.44$, $p < .01$, and the revised model provided an acceptable fit to the data. After the initial, and specified a priori, addition to the model, there were no modifications suggested by the results.

Sample Results Section

As in the previous chapter, a sample results section based on the preceding analyses is presented below.

Results

Descriptive statistics and intercorrelations for all study variables are presented in Table 6.1. All model tests were based on the covariance matrix and used maximum likelihood estimation as implemented in LISREL VIII (Jöreskog & Sörbom, 1992).

The original model provided an adequate but not outstanding fit to the data [$\chi^2(5) = 33.24$, $p < .01$; GFI = .94; AGFI = .83; RMSEA = .17; NFI = .91; CFI = .92; PNFI = .45]. The revised model provided

TABLE 6.1 Descriptive Statistics and Intercorrelations (n = 202)

	Mean	SD	1	2	3	4
1. Participation	2.62	1.71	1.00			
2. Willingness to work for the union	10.32	3.88	0.47	1.00		
3. Union loyalty	20.00	5.55	0.39	0.71	1.00	
4. Instrumentality beliefs	19.87	5.60	0.29	0.48	0.61	1.00
5. Subjective norms	18.09	9.99	0.29	0.53	0.51	0.39

a better fit to the data than did the original model, $\chi^2_{\text{difference}}(1) = 30.44$, $p < .01$; $\chi^2(4) = 2.80$, ns; GFI = .99; AGFI = .98; RMSEA = .00; NFI = .99; CFI = 1.00; PNFI = .40.

Standardized parameter estimates for the revised model are presented in Figure 6.4. As shown, participation in union activities was predicted by willingness to work for the union ($\beta = .47$, $p < .01$), which in turn was predicted by both union loyalty ($\beta = .60$, $p < .01$) and subjective norms ($\beta = .22$, $p < .01$). Union loyalty was predicted by both perceptions of instrumentality ($\beta = .49$, $p < .01$) and subjective norms ($\beta = .32$, $p < .01$). The model explained 22% of the variance in participation, 54% of the variance in willingness to work for the union, and 46% of the variance in union loyalty.

Note

1. Rank and order conditions refer to the identification of nonrecursive structural models and will not be dealt with further.

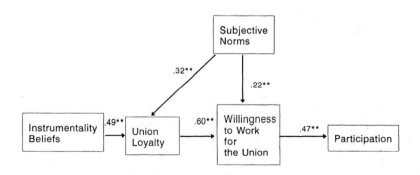

Figure 6.4.

CHAPTER 7

Latent Variable Path Analysis

The true power of structural equation modeling is the ability to estimate a complete model incorporating both measurement and structural considerations. In this chapter, we consider such a latent variable path analysis. Latent variable path analysis uses the full LISREL model (all eight matrices) to combine measurement and structural considerations. Thus, in conducting the analysis we will be equally concerned with assessing the proposed measurement relations (i.e., through confirmatory factor analysis) and the proposed structural relations (i.e., through path analysis).

Model Specification

To illustrate the use of latent variable path analysis, we will consider a reduced form of the model of perceived risk and participation in occupational health and safety programs presented by Cree and Kelloway (in press). There are two components to the model. First, the structural model specifies the predictive relationships among the latent variables. Second, the measurement model defines how the latent variables are measured (i.e., represented by indicators).

The structural model we were interested in was based on the hypotheses that two factors, perceived health and safety climate and accident history, predicted perceived risk in the workplace, which in turn predicted willingness to participate in health and safety programs (see Figure 7.1).

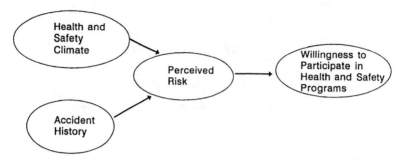

Figure 7.1.

In addition to the structural relations, we also were interested in using latent variables; that is, each construct in the model would be represented by multiple indicators. Bentler (1980, p. 425) notes that

> choosing the right number of indicators for each LV [latent variable] is something of an art; in principle, the more the better; in practice, too many indicators make it difficult if not impossible to fit a model to data.

Moreover, as noted in Chapter 5, Bollen (1989) has suggested that a confirmatory factor analysis model (which uses indicators to represent latent variables or factors) should incorporate at least two indicators per latent variable. For each construct (latent variable) in the model, therefore, we attempted to identify at least two observed indicators (actual items).

Specifically, perceived health and safety climate was assessed with three scales that asked respondents to rate their perceptions of their manager's, supervisor's, and coworkers' commitment to health and safety in the workplace. Accident history was assessed by two questionnaires: one asking about the respondent's own history with accidents in the workplace and the other asking whether respondents had heard about or witnessed accidents in the workplace.

The endogenous variables also were measured with multiple indicators. Perceived risk in the workplace was measured by two questionnaires asking respondents how risky they thought the workplace was (a) for them personally and (b) for their coworkers. Finally, willingness to participate in health and safety programs was measured by a 12-item questionnaire assessing respondents' willingness to participate in a

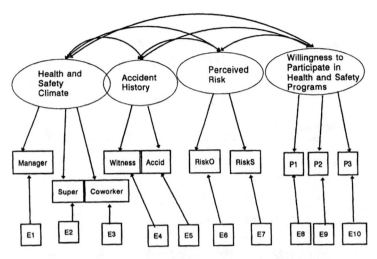

Figure 7.2.

variety of health and safety programs. Because we wanted to generate multiple indicators for this construct, we randomly assigned items to one of three indicator variables (i.e., three subscales with four items per scale). The measurement model described above is given in Figure 7.2. Integrating the structural and measurement models results in the full latent variable path analysis model given in Figure 7.3.

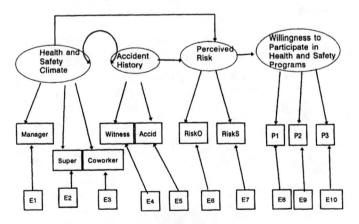

Figure 7.3.

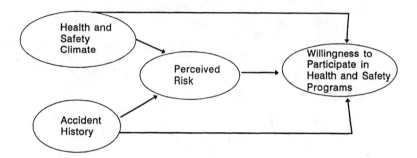

Figure 7.4.

Alternative Model Specifications

The central hypothesis of our model is that risk perceptions mediate the relationships between health and safety climate and accident history, as the predictors, and willingness to participate in health and safety programs in the workplace, as the outcome. Consistent with the discussion of mediated relationships in the previous chapter, two plausible rival model specifications are the partially mediated (which adds paths from the two predictors to willingness to participate, see Figure 7.4) and nonmediated (which deletes the path from risk perception to willingness to participate, see Figure 7.5) models.

Model Testing Strategy

There is a major complication in testing latent variable models. If the model does not fit, the lack of fit can be attributable to (a) an ill-fitting

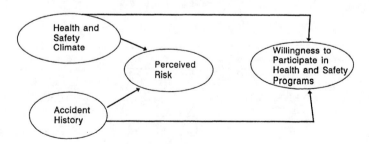

Figure 7.5.

measurement model, (b) an ill-fitting structural model, or (c) both (Anderson & Gerbing, 1988). Accordingly, Anderson and Gerbing recommend a strategy of two-stage modeling in which one first assesses the fit of the measurement model and then moves to a consideration of the structural model.

The strategy is based on the observation that the latent variable structural model incorporates the measurement model. In fact, at least with respect to the relationships among the latent variables, one can think of the measurement model as a saturated or just-identified model. That is, the measurement model allows a relationship (i.e., a correlation, see Figure 7.2) between each pair of latent variables.

This being the case, the fit of the measurement model provides a baseline for the fit of the full latent variable model. The full model, incorporating both structural and measurement relationships, cannot provide a better fit to the data than does the measurement model.

Incorporating Anderson and Gerbing's (1988) suggestions with our three hypothesized structural models suggests a sequence of model tests in which we first establish the fit of the measurement model and then move to a consideration of the structural parameters of interest. The remainder of this chapter, therefore, provides the assessment of the measurement model, followed by assessment of the full model.

From Pictures to LISREL

The translation of the path diagrams proceeds just as in previous examples. First, we will translate the measurement model. For purposes of illustration, we will assess the measurement model on the endogenous (Y) side of the LISREL model. (Note that it should not matter whether one operationalizes the factor analysis on the endogenous or exogenous side of the model.)

Operationalizing a confirmatory factor analysis on the endogenous side of the LISREL model still requires that you specify a scale of measurement for the latent variables. Recall that in Chapter 5 we specified the scale of measurement by declaring PH = ST, which assigned the latent variables to be standardized. This option is not available on the endogenous side of the model (you cannot declare PS = ST). The scale of measurement therefore is assigned by fixing one of the latent variable-indicator paths to equal 1.0 for each latent variable. In effect, this specification tells LISREL that the latent variable is on the same scale of measurement as the indicator. It should not make a great deal of difference which indicator is chosen to represent the scale of measure-

TABLE 7.1 Lambda Y (Factor Loadings for Y)

	Health and Safety Climate	Accident History	Perceived Risk	Willingness to Participate
1. Manager commitment	1.00	FIxed	FIxed	FIxed
2. Supervisor commitment	FRee	FIxed	FIxed	FIxed
3. Coworker commitment	FRee	FIxed	FIxed	FIxed
4. Own accident history	FIxed	1.00	FIxed	FIxed
5. Witnessed accidents	FIxed	FRee	FIxed	FIxed
6. Risk for self	FIxed	FIxed	1.00	FIxed
7. Risk for others	FIxed	FIxed	FRee	FIxed
8. Participate 1	FIxed	FIxed	FIxed	1.00
9. Participate 2	FIxed	FIxed	FIxed	FRee
10. Participate 3	FIxed	FIxed	FIxed	FRee

ment for the latent variable (assuming that the indicators are all measured along a similar scale).

The forms of the three matrices (**LY, PS,** and **TE**) are presented below. Because there are four latent variables with ten indicators, **LY** will have four columns and ten rows. **PS** will be a 4 × 4 symmetric matrix. Note that **PS** has all elements freed; that is, we are going to estimate both the variances for the latent variables and the covariances among the latent variables. Because we will again assume that there are no correlated errors of measurement among the indicator variables, **TE** is declared to be diagonal and free; that is, **TE** is a vector with ten elements (one for each observed variable).

Identification and Estimation

The model meets Bollen's (1989) criteria for identification. That is, each latent variable has at least two indicators, and the latent variables are

TABLE 7.2 PSI (Covariances for E)

	Health and Safety Climate	Accident History	Perceived Risk	Willingness to Participate
1. Health and safety climate	FRee			
2. Accident history	FRee	FRee		
3. Perceived risk	FRee	FRee	FRee	
4. Willingness to participate	FRee	FRee	FRee	FRee

TABLE 7.3 TE (Unique Factors for the Endogenous Variables)

1. Manager commitment	FRee
2. Supervisor commitment	FRee
3. Coworker commitment	FRee
4. Own accident history	FRee
5. Witnessed accidents	FRee
6. Risk for self	FRee
7. Risk for others	FRee
8. Participate 1	FRee
9. Participate 2	FRee
10. Participate 3	FRee

allowed to correlate freely with one another. Moreover, like all confirmatory factor analysis models, the model is recursive. (The causal flow is always from the latent variables to the observed indicators.)

The source code used to estimate the model is given below.

```
TI MEASUREMENT MODEL
DA NI = 13 NO = 115 MA = CM
```

Note: There are 10 indicators and 115 observations, and I want to analyze the covariance matrix.

```
ME
    10.7 8.9 10.9 18.6 3.8 5.5 5.7 5.5 1.7 0.9
```

Note: These are the item means.

```
SD
    2.7 3.1 2.9 7.3 1.5 1.4 1.2 1.2 1.7 0.8
```

Note: These are the item standard deviations.

```
KM SY
    1.00
     .76  1.00
     .78   .68  1.00
    -.05   .01  -.05  1.00
     .10   .09   .08   .52  1.00
     .01   .08   .14  -.28  -.22  1.00
```

```
        .20    .18    .29   -.44   -.29    .54   1.00
        .22    .25    .29   -.42   -.31    .57    .65   1.00
        .00    .00   -.05    .42    .22   -.13   -.26   -.20   1.00
        .12    .03    .11    .26    .30   -.12   -.20   -.17    .47
  1.00
```

Note: This is the lower half of the correlation matrix.

```
LA
   p1 p2 p3 risks riskc mgr super cow own witness
```

Note: These are variable labels for the indicator variables.

```
MO NY = 10 NE = 4 PS = SY,FR
```

Note: The model declares 10 indicators and 4 latent variables. By declaring NY and NE, LISREL selects a confirmatory factor analysis on the endogenous side of the model involving matrices **LY**, **PS**, and **TE**.

```
LE
   part risk climate accid
```

Note: These are labels for the latent variables.

```
VA 1.0 LY(1,1) LY(4,2) LY(6,3) LY(9,4)
```

Note: This statement inserts the value 1.0 in the designated locations, thereby declaring a scale for the latent variables. Recall that matrix **LY** has all elements FIxed by default, so no further specification is necessary.

```
FR LY(2,1) LY(3,1) LY(5,2) LY(7,3) LY(8,3) LY(10,4)
```

Note: Frees the remaining parameters specified in the measurement model.

```
OU ML SC TV MI
```

Note: Asks for maximum likelihood estimation. I want to see the completely standardized solution, the t values, and the modification indices.

Edited Output

```
NUMBER OF INPUT VARIABLES 10
NUMBER OF Y - VARIABLES   10
NUMBER OF X - VARIABLES    0
NUMBER OF ETA - VARIABLES  4
NUMBER OF KSI - VARIABLES  0
NUMBER OF OBSERVATIONS   115
```

COVARIANCE MATRIX TO BE ANALYZED

	p1	p2	p3	risks	riskc	plant
p1	7.30					
p2	6.27	9.27				
p3	6.05	5.93	8.21			
risks	-1.03	0.20	-1.11	53.60		
riskc	0.40	0.43	0.34	5.68	2.23	
plant	0.04	0.35	0.59	-2.99	-0.47	2.08
super	0.67	0.67	1.03	-3.97	-0.54	0.96
cow	0.70	0.90	0.98	-3.61	-0.54	0.96
dir	-0.02	-0.01	-0.24	5.21	0.55	-0.31
vic	0.26	0.08	0.25	1.53	0.36	-0.14

COVARIANCE MATRIX TO BE ANALYZED

	super	cow	dir	vic
super	1.55			
cow	0.95	1.39		
dir	-0.55	-0.39	2.82	
vic	-0.20	-0.17	0.64	0.66

PARAMETER SPECIFICATIONS

LAMBDA-Y

	part	risk	climate	accid
p1	0	0	0	0
p2	1	0	0	0
p3	2	0	0	0
risks	0	0	0	0
riskc	0	3	0	0
plant	0	0	0	0
super	0	0	4	0

cow	0	0	5	0
dir	0	0	0	0
vic	0	0	0	6

PSI

	part	risk	climate	accid
part	7			
risk	8	9		
climate	10	11	12	
accid	13	14	15	16

THETA-EPS

p1	p2	p3	risks	riskc	plant
17	18	19	20	21	22

THETA-EPS

super	cow	dir	vic
23	24	25	26

Number of Iterations = 9

LISREL ESTIMATES (MAXIMUM LIKELIHOOD)
LAMBDA-Y

	part	risk	climate	accid
p1	1.00	- -	- -	- -
p2	1.00	- -	- -	- -
	(0.09)			
	11.18			
p3	0.97	- -	- -	- -
	(0.08)			
	11.68			
risks	- -	1.00	- -	- -
riskc	- -	0.15	- -	- -
		(0.03)		
		4.93		
plant	- -	- -	1.00	- -
super	- -	- -	1.05	- -
			(0.16)	
			6.68	
cow	- -	- -	1.03	- -
			(0.15)	
			6.75	

```
dir           - -        - -        - -        1.00
vic           - -        - -        - -        0.37
                                              (0.10)
                                               3.62
```

COVARIANCE MATRIX OF ETA

	part	risk	climate	accid
part	6.22			
risk	-0.14	38.39		
climate	0.68	-3.51	0.90	
accid	0.10	4.84	-0.43	1.73

PSI

	part	risk	climate	accid
part	6.22			
	(1.01)			
	6.14			
risk	-0.14	38.39		
	(1.74)	(9.44)		
	-0.08	4.07		
climate	0.68	-3.51	0.90	
	(0.27)	(0.88)	(0.25)	
	2.46	-4.00	3.63	
accid	0.10	4.84	-0.43	1.73
	(0.39)	(1.22)	(0.17)	(0.56)
	0.26	3.97	-2.53	3.09

THETA-EPS

p1	p2	p3	risks	riskc	plant
1.07	3.04	2.34	15.20	1.39	1.19
(0.36)	(0.53)	(0.44)	(6.84)	(0.23)	(0.19)
2.95	5.78	5.27	2.22	5.95	6.41

THETA-EPS

super	cow	dir	vic
0.55	0.44	1.09	0.43
(0.12)	(0.11)	(0.46)	(0.08)
4.63	4.10	2.33	5.13

```
SQUARED MULTIPLE CORRELATIONS FOR Y - VARIABLES
    p1       p2       p3      risks     riskc    plant
   ____     ____     ____     ____      ____     ____

   0.85     0.67     0.72     0.72      0.38     0.43

SQUARED MULTIPLE CORRELATIONS FOR Y - VARIABLES
   super     cow      dir      vic
   ____     ____     ____     ____

   0.64     0.68     0.61     0.36
```

GOODNESS OF FIT STATISTICS

```
            CHI-SQUARE WITH 29 DEGREES OF FREEDOM =   30.89 (P = 0.37)
     ESTIMATED NON-CENTRALITY PARAMETER (NCP) =    1.89
       90 PERCENT CONFIDENCE INTERVAL FOR NCP =   (0.0 ; 19.50)
                 MINIMUM FIT FUNCTION VALUE =    0.27
   POPULATION DISCREPANCY FUNCTION VALUE (F0) =    0.017
        90 PERCENT CONFIDENCE INTERVAL FOR F0 =   (0.0 ; 0.17)
ROOT MEAN SQUARE ERROR OF APPROXIMATION (RMSEA) =    0.024
      90 PERCENT CONFIDENCE INTERVAL FOR RMSEA =   (0.0 ; 0.077)
    P-VALUE FOR TEST OF CLOSE FIT (RMSEA < 0.05) =    0.73
         EXPECTED CROSS-VALIDATION INDEX (ECVI) =    0.73
        90 PERCENT CONFIDENCE INTERVAL FOR ECVI =   (0.71 ; 0.88)
                     ECVI FOR SATURATED MODEL =    0.96
                  ECVI FOR INDEPENDENCE MODEL =    4.41
   CHI-SQUARE FOR INDEPENDENCE MODEL WITH 45
                          DEGREES OF FREEDOM = 482.66
                         INDEPENDENCE AIC = 502.66
                                MODEL AIC =  82.89
                            SATURATED AIC = 110.00
                       INDEPENDENCE CAIC = 540.11
                              MODEL CAIC = 180.26
                          SATURATED CAIC = 315.97
              ROOT MEAN SQUARE RESIDUAL (RMR) =    0.27
                          STANDARDIZED RMR  =    0.050
                   GOODNESS OF FIT INDEX (GFI) =    0.95
        ADJUSTED GOODNESS OF FIT INDEX (AGFI) =    0.90
      PARSIMONY GOODNESS OF FIT INDEX (PGFI) =    0.50
                        NORMED FIT INDEX (NFI) =    0.94
                   NON-NORMED FIT INDEX (NNFI) =    0.99
           PARSIMONY NORMED FIT INDEX (PNFI) =    0.60
                  COMPARATIVE FIT INDEX (CFI) =    1.00
                  INCREMENTAL FIT INDEX (IFI) =    1.00
```

```
RELATIVE FIT INDEX (RFI) =   0.90
CRITICAL N (CN) = 184.00
```

MODIFICATION INDICES AND EXPECTED CHANGE MODIFICATION
INDICES FOR LAMBDA-Y

	part	risk	climate	accid
p1	- -	0.02	2.74	0.28
p2	- -	0.39	0.00	0.00
p3	- -	0.54	3.56	0.38
risks	2.51	- -	0.12	0.22
riskc	2.51	- -	0.12	0.22
plant	3.42	0.64	- -	0.60
super	0.15	0.79	- -	1.47
cow	1.01	0.05	- -	0.36
dir	1.75	1.84	0.01	- -
vic	1.75	1.84	0.01	- -

EXPECTED CHANGE FOR LAMBDA-Y

	part	risk	climate	accid
p1	- -	0.00	-0.30	0.07
p2	- -	0.02	0.00	0.00
p3	- -	-0.02	0.38	-0.09
risks	-0.55	- -	-0.63	0.63
riskc	0.08	- -	0.09	-0.09
plant	-0.09	0.02	- -	0.09
super	0.02	-0.02	- -	-0.11
cow	0.04	0.01	- -	0.05
dir	-0.11	0.72	0.02	- -
vic	0.04	-0.27	-0.01	- -

STANDARDIZED EXPECTED CHANGE FOR LAMBDA-Y

	part	risk	climate	accid
p1	- -	0.02	-0.28	0.09
p2	- -	0.13	0.00	0.00
p3	- -	-0.14	0.36	-0.12
risks	-1.38	- -	-0.59	0.83
riskc	0.20	- -	0.09	-0.12
plant	-0.23	0.14	- -	0.11

super	0.04	-0.14	- -	-0.15
cow	0.10	0.03	- -	0.07
dir	-0.27	4.46	0.02	- -
vic	0.10	-1.66	-0.01	- -

COMPLETELY STANDARDIZED EXPECTED CHANGE FOR LAMBDA-Y

	part	risk	climate	accid
p1	- -	0.01	-0.10	0.03
p2	- -	0.04	0.00	0.00
p3	- -	-0.05	0.13	-0.04
risks	-0.19	- -	-0.08	0.11
riskc	0.14	- -	0.06	-0.08
plant	-0.16	0.10	- -	0.08
super	0.03	-0.11	- -	-0.12
cow	0.08	0.03	- -	0.06
dir	-0.16	2.66	0.01	- -
vic	0.12	-2.03	-0.01	- -

NO NON-ZERO MODIFICATION INDICES FOR PSI

MODIFICATION INDICES FOR THETA-EPS

	p1	p2	p3	risks	riskc	plant
p1	- -					
p2	4.07	- -				
p3	0.24	4.67	- -			
risks	3.32	1.24	0.13	- -		
riskc	0.28	0.00	0.25	- -	- -	
plant	5.22	0.17	0.87	0.99	0.02	- -
super	0.01	0.97	1.42	0.28	0.05	0.28
cow	0.18	1.38	0.00	0.00	0.25	1.54
dir	0.01	0.20	1.08	5.47	4.24	0.45
vic	0.88	1.81	1.24	4.94	3.74	0.02

MODIFICATION INDICES FOR THETA-EPS

	super	cow	dir	vic
super	- -			
cow	4.18	- -		
dir	0.59	0.57	- -	
vic	0.06	0.10	- -	- -

EXPECTED CHANGE FOR THETA-EPS

	p1	p2	p3	risks	riskc	plant
p1	- -					
p2	2.80	- -				
p3	0.71	-2.54	- -			
risks	-1.46	1.13	0.33	- -		
riskc	0.09	0.00	0.10	- -	- -	
plant	-0.37	0.09	0.18	0.63	-0.02	- -
super	0.01	-0.16	0.17	-0.27	0.02	0.08
cow	-0.05	0.17	0.01	0.02	-0.05	0.17
dir	-0.02	0.11	-0.24	2.66	-0.39	0.10
vic	0.09	-0.17	0.13	-1.10	0.17	-0.01

EXPECTED CHANGE FOR THETA-EPS

	super	cow	dir	vic
super	- -			
cow	-0.35	- -		
dir	-0.09	0.09	- -	
vic	-0.01	-0.02	- -	- -

COMPLETELY STANDARDIZED EXPECTED CHANGE FOR THETA-EPS

	p1	p2	p3	risks	riskc	plant
p1	- -					
p2	0.34	- -				
p3	0.09	-0.29	- -			
risks	-0.07	0.05	0.02	- -		
riskc	0.02	0.00	0.02	- -	- -	
plant	-0.09	0.02	0.04	0.06	-0.01	- -
super	0.00	-0.04	0.05	-0.03	0.01	0.04
cow	-0.02	0.05	0.00	0.00	-0.03	0.10
dir	0.00	0.02	-0.05	0.22	-0.16	0.04
vic	0.04	-0.07	0.06	-0.18	0.14	-0.01

COMPLETELY STANDARDIZED EXPECTED CHANGE FOR THETA-EPS

	super	cow	dir	vic
super	- -			
cow	-0.24	- -		
dir	-0.04	0.04	- -	
vic	-0.01	-0.02	- -	- -

MAXIMUM MODIFICATION INDEX IS 5.47 FOR ELEMENT (9, 4) OF
THETA-EPS
STANDARDIZED SOLUTION
LAMBDA-Y

	part	risk	climate	accid
p1	2.49	- -	- -	- -
p2	2.50	- -	- -	- -
p3	2.42	- -	- -	- -
risks	- -	6.20	- -	- -
riskc	- -	0.92	- -	- -
plant	- -	- -	0.95	- -
super	- -	- -	1.00	- -
cow	- -	- -	0.98	- -
dir	- -	- -	- -	1.32
vic	- -	- -	- -	0.49

CORRELATION MATRIX OF ETA

	part	risk	climate	accid
part	1.00			
risk	-0.01	1.00		
climate	0.29	-0.60	1.00	
accid	0.03	0.59	-0.35	1.00

PSI

	part	risk	climate	accid
part	1.00			
risk	-0.01	1.00		
climate	0.29	-0.60	1.00	
accid	0.03	0.59	-0.35	1.00

COMPLETELY STANDARDIZED SOLUTION
LAMBDA-Y

	part	risk	climate	accid
p1	0.92	- -	- -	- -
p2	0.82	- -	- -	- -
p3	0.85	- -	- -	- -
risks	- -	0.85	- -	- -

riskc	- -	0.61	- -	- -
plant	- -	- -	0.66	- -
super	- -	- -	0.80	- -
cow	- -	- -	0.83	- -
dir	- -	- -	- -	0.78
vic	- -	- -	- -	0.60

CORRELATION MATRIX OF ETA

	part	risk	climate	accid
part	1.00			
risk	-0.01	1.00		
climate	0.29	-0.60	1.00	
accid	0.03	0.59	-0.35	1.00

PSI

	part	risk	climate	accid
part	1.00			
risk	-0.01	1.00		
climate	0.29	-0.60	1.00	
accid	0.03	0.59	-0.35	1.00

THETA-EPS

p1	p2	p3	risks	riskc	plant
0.15	0.33	0.28	0.28	0.6	0.57

THETA-EPS

super	cow	dir	vic
0.36	0.32	0.39	0.64

Assessment and Modification

As specified, the measurement model provides an acceptable fit to the data [$\chi^2(29)$ = 30.89, ns; GFI = .95; AGFI = .90; RMSEA = .02; NFI = .94; CFI = 1.00; PNFI = .60; PGFI = .50], and all estimated parameters are significant. We can proceed, therefore, with the assessment of the structural model.

From Pictures to LISREL

Although the measurement model was estimated entirely on the endogenous side of the LISREL model, the full latent variable model requires the use of both the exogenous and endogenous sides of the model. We begin by setting up the measurement of the exogenous and endogenous variables (thereby using both methods of setting a scale of measurement for the latent variables) and then proceed to set up the structural model. The setups are shown in Tables 7.4–7.11.

Note that the correlation between risk and willingness to participate is fixed in the PS matrix (PS 2, 1). Recall that PS appears in both the measurement model for the endogenous variables and the structural model. Because we are estimating a path between risk and willingness to participate [BE (2, 1], we cannot simultaneously estimate the correlation between the two factors. Thus, PS takes the form appropriate for the structural model.

TABLE 7.4 LX (Factor Loading for Exogenous Variables)

	Health and Safety Climate	Accident History
1. Manager's commitment	FRee	FIxed
2. Supervisor's commitment	FRee	FIxed
3. Coworker's commitment	FRee	FIxed
4. Own accident history	FIxed	FRee
5. Witnessed accidents	FIxed	FRee

Table 7.5 PH (Factor Covariances for Exogenous Variables)

	Health and Safety Climate	Accident History
1. Health and safety climate	1.00	
2. Accident history	FRee	1.00

TABLE 7.6 TD (Unique Factors for Exogenous Variables)

1. Manager's commitment	FRee
2. Supervisor's commitment	FRee
3. Coworker's commitment	FRee
4. Own accident history	FRee
5. Witnessed accidents	FRee

TABLE 7.7 LY (Factor Loadings for Endogenous Variables)

	Risk	*Willingness to Participate*
1. Risk for self	1.00	FIxed
2. Risk for Coworkers	FRee	FIxed
3. Participation 1	FIxed	1.00
4. Participation 2	FIxed	FRee
5. Participation 3	FIxed	FRee

TABLE 7.8 TE (Unique Factors for Endogenous Variables)

1. Risk for self	FRee
2. Risk for coworkers	FRee
3. Participation 1	FRee
4. Participation 2	FRee
5. Participation 3	FRee

TABLE 7.9 GA (Relates Exogenous to Endogenous Variables)

	Health and Safety Climate	*Accident History*
1. Risk	FRee	FRee
2. Willingness to participate	FIxed	FIxed

TABLE 7.10 BE (Relates Endogenous to Endogenous Variables)

	Risk	*Willingness to Participate*
1. Risk	FIxed	FIxed
2. Willingness to participate	FRee	FIxed

TABLE 7.11 PS (Factor Covariances for Endogenous Variables)

	Risk	*Willingness to Participate*
1. Risk	FRee	
2. Willingness to participate	FIxed	FRee

Identification and Estimation II

The measurement relationships incorporated in the model have not changed from the previous analysis; therefore, the measurement component of the model is identified. Because the structural model involves only recursive relationships, the structural component also is identified (Bollen, 1989).

The source code used to estimate the model is given below.

```
DA NI = 10 NO = 115 MA = CM
ME
      10.7 8.9 10.9 18.6 3.8 5.5 5.7 5.5 1.7  0.9

SD
      2.7 3.1 2.9 7.3 1.5 1.4 1.2 1.2 1.7  0.8

KM SY
1.00
 .76  1.00
 .78   .68  1.00
-.05   .01  -.05  1.00
 .10   .09   .08   .52  1.00
 .01   .08   .14  -.28  -.22  1.00
 .20   .18   .29  -.44  -.29   .54  1.00
 .22   .25   .29  -.42  -.31   .57   .65  1.00
 .00   .00  -.05   .42   .22  -.13  -.26  -.20  1.00
 .12   .03   .11   .26   .30  -.12  -.20  -.17   .47  1.00

LA
p1 p2 p3 risks riskc plant super cow dir vic
MO NY = 5 NE = 2 NK = 2 NX = 5 PS = DI,FR PH = ST GA = FU,FI BE = FU,FI

LE
   part risk

LK
   climate accid
FR GA(2,1) GA(2,2) BE(1,2)
VA 1.0 LY(1,1) LY(4,2)
FR LY(2,1) LY(3,1) LY(5,2)
FR LX(1,1) LX(2,1) LX(3,1) LX(4,2) LX(5,2)
OU ML SC TV MI
```

Edited Output

```
NUMBER OF INPUT VARIABLES 10
NUMBER OF Y - VARIABLES    5
NUMBER OF X - VARIABLES    5
NUMBER OF ETA - VARIABLES  2
NUMBER OF KSI - VARIABLES  2
NUMBER OF OBSERVATIONS    115
```

PARAMETER SPECIFICATIONS

LAMBDA-Y

	part	risk
p1	0	0
p2	1	0
p3	2	0
risks	0	0
riskc	0	3

LAMBDA-X

	climate	accid
plant	4	0
super	5	0
cow	6	0
dir	0	7
vic	0	8

BETA

	part	risk
part	0	9
risk	0	0

GAMMA

	climate	accid
part	0	0
risk	10	11

PHI

	climate	accid
climate	0	
accid	12	0

PSI

part	risk
13	14

THETA-EPS

p1	p2	p3	risks	riskc
15	16	17	18	19

THETA-DELTA

plant	super	cow	dir	vic
20	21	22	23	24

LISREL ESTIMATES (MAXIMUM LIKELIHOOD)

LAMBDA-Y

	part	risk
p1	1.00	- -
p2	0.98	- -
	(0.09)	
	11.06	
p3	0.95	- -
	(0.08)	
	11.48	
risks	- -	1.00
riskc	- -	0.14
		(0.03)
		4.67

LAMBDA-X

	climate	accid
plant	0.97	- -
	(0.13)	
	7.43	
super	0.99	- -
	(0.11)	
	9.19	

cow	0.97 (0.10) 9.45	- -
dir	- -	1.37 (0.22) 6.15
vic	- -	0.47 (0.09) 5.00

BETA

	part	risk
part	- -	-0.02 (0.04) -0.51
risk	- -	- -

GAMMA

	climate	accid
part	- -	- -
risk	-2.86 (0.72) -3.99	2.69 (0.78) 3.44

COVARIANCE MATRIX OF ETA AND KSI

	part	risk	climate	accid
part	6.39			
risk	-0.89	41.09		
climate	0.08	-3.77	1.00	
accid	-0.08	3.65	-0.34	1.00

PHI

	climate	accid
climate	1.00	
accid	-0.34 (0.12) -2.91	1.00

PSI

part	risk
6.37	20.48

```
        (1.02)    (8.04)
         6.25      2.55
```

SQUARED MULTIPLE CORRELATIONS FOR STRUCTURAL EQUATIONS
        part   risk
        ────   ────

        0.00   0.50

THETA-EPS

p1	p2	p3	risks	riskc
0.90	3.13	2.48	12.51	1.45
(0.38)	(0.54)	(0.46)	(7.52)	(0.24)
2.41	5.83	5.41	1.66	6.11

SQUARED MULTIPLE CORRELATIONS FOR Y - VARIABLES

p1	p2	p3	risks	riskc
0.88	0.66	0.70	0.77	0.35

THETA-DELTA

plant	super	cow	dir	vic
1.15	0.56	0.46	0.93	0.45
(0.18)	(0.12)	(0.11)	(0.52)	(0.08)
6.25	4.51	4.14	1.80	5.37

SQUARED MULTIPLE CORRELATIONS FOR X - VARIABLES

plant	super	cow	dir	vic
0.45	0.64	0.67	0.67	0.33

GOODNESS OF FIT STATISTICS
```
                   CHI-SQUARE WITH 31 DEGREES OF FREEDOM =  39.60 (P = 0.14)
             ESTIMATED NON-CENTRALITY PARAMETER (NCP) =   8.60
             90 PERCENT CONFIDENCE INTERVAL FOR NCP =  (0.0 ; 28.92)
                          MINIMUM FIT FUNCTION VALUE =   0.35
       POPULATION DISCREPANCY FUNCTION VALUE (F0) =   0.075
                90 PERCENT CONFIDENCE INTERVAL FOR F0 =  (0.0 ; 0.25)
 ROOT MEAN SQUARE ERROR OF APPROXIMATION (RMSEA) =   0.049
           90 PERCENT CONFIDENCE INTERVAL FOR RMSEA =  (0.0 ; 0.090)
   P-VALUE FOR TEST OF CLOSE FIT (RMSEA < 0.05) =   0.48
           EXPECTED CROSS-VALIDATION INDEX (ECVI) =   0.77
              90 PERCENT CONFIDENCE INTERVAL FOR ECVI =  (0.69 ; 0.95)
```

```
                    ECVI FOR SATURATED MODEL =    0.96
                 ECVI FOR INDEPENDENCE MODEL =    4.41
  CHI-SQUARE FOR INDEPENDENCE MODEL WITH 45
                         DEGREES OF FREEDOM = 482.66
                          INDEPENDENCE AIC = 502.66
                                 MODEL AIC =  87.60
                             SATURATED AIC = 110.00
                          INDEPENDENCE CAIC = 540.11
                                MODEL CAIC = 177.48
                             SATURATED CAIC = 315.97
             ROOT MEAN SQUARE RESIDUAL (RMR) =    0.35
                           STANDARDIZED RMR =    0.087
                 GOODNESS OF FIT INDEX (GFI) =    0.94
        ADJUSTED GOODNESS OF FIT INDEX (AGFI) =    0.89
       PARSIMONY GOODNESS OF FIT INDEX (PGFI) =    0.53
                    NORMED FIT INDEX (NFI) =    0.92
                NON-NORMED FIT INDEX (NNFI) =    0.97
          PARSIMONY NORMED FIT INDEX (PNFI) =    0.63
              COMPARATIVE FIT INDEX (CFI) =    0.98
             INCREMENTAL FIT INDEX (IFI) =    0.98
                RELATIVE FIT INDEX (RFI) =    0.88
                          CRITICAL N (CN) = 151.25
```

MODIFICATION INDICES AND EXPECTED CHANGE
MODIFICATION INDICES FOR LAMBDA-Y

	part	risk
p1	- -	0.00
p2	- -	0.45
p3	- -	0.42
risks	0.01	- -
riskc	3.50	- -

MODIFICATION INDICES FOR LAMBDA-X

	climate	accid
plant	- -	0.95
super	- -	1.62
cow	- -	0.23
dir	0.23	- -
vic	0.23	- -

```
MODIFICATION INDICES FOR BETA
               part        risk
               ____        ____

part           - -         - -
risk           3.28        - -
```

```
MODIFICATION INDICES FOR GAMMA
               climate     accid
               ____        ____

part           7.84        0.30
risk           - -         - -
```

NO NONZERO MODIFICATION INDICES FOR PHI

```
MODIFICATION INDICES FOR PSI
               part        risk
               ____        ____

part           - -
risk           3.28        - -
```

MODIFICATION INDICES FOR THETA-EPS

	p1	p2	p3	risks	riskc
p1	- -				
p2	0.42	- -			
p3	0.45	0.00	- -		
risks	2.05	1.70	0.39	- -	
riskc	0.44	0.00	0.21	3.28	- -

MODIFICATION INDICES FOR THETA-DELTA-EPS

	p1	p2	p3	risks	riskc
plant	3.92	0.39	1.13	0.72	0.03
super	0.17	0.68	1.49	0.21	0.09
cow	0.00	1.73	0.06	0.00	0.14
dir	0.02	0.22	0.88	3.66	3.66
vic	0.92	1.69	1.07	3.87	4.58

MAXIMUM MODIFICATION INDEX IS 7.84 FOR ELEMENT (1, 1) OF GAMMA
COMPLETELY STANDARDIZED SOLUTION
LAMBDA-Y

```
               part        risk
               ____        ____

p1             0.94        - -
```

p2	0.81	- -
p3	0.84	- -
risks	- -	0.88
riskc	- -	0.59

LAMBDA-X

	climate	accid
plant	0.67	- -
super	0.80	- -
cow	0.82	- -
dir	- -	0.82
vic	- -	0.57

BETA

	part	risk
part	- -	-0.06
risk	- -	- -

GAMMA

	climate	accid
part	- -	- -
risk	-0.45	0.42

CORRELATION MATRIX OF ETA AND KSI

	part	risk	climate	accid
part	1.00			
risk	-0.06	1.00		
climate	0.03	-0.59	1.00	
accid	-0.03	0.57	-0.34	1.00

PSI

part	risk
1.00	0.50

THETA-EPS

p1	p2	p3	risks	riskc
0.12	0.34	0.30	0.23	0.65

THETA-DELTA

plant	super	cow	dir	vic
0.55	0.36	0.33	0.33	0.67

REGRESSION MATRIX ETA ON KSI (STANDARDIZED)

	climate	accid
part	0.02	-0.02
risk	-0.45	0.42

Assessment and Modification II

This is an interesting case in that although the model provides an acceptable fit to the data [$\chi^2(31)$ = 39.60, ns; GFI = .94; AGFI = .89; RMSEA = .05; NFI = .92; CFI = .98; PNFI = .63; PGFI = .53], not all the paths in the model are significant. Risk perceptions do not significantly predict willingness to participate (β = −.06, ns).

The partially mediated model (resulting from adding paths from both exogenous variables to willingness to participate) provided a significantly better fit to the data [$\chi^2_{difference}(2)$ = 8.72, p < .02; $\chi^2(29)$ = 30.89, ns; GFI = .95; AGFI = .90; RMSEA = .02; NFI = .94; CFI = 1.00; PNFI = .60; PGFI = .50]. The nonmediated model (which deletes the path from risk perceptions to willingness) also provided a good fit to the data [$\chi^2(30)$ = 32.07, ns; GFI = .95; AGFI = .90; RMSEA = .03; NFI = .93; CFI = 1.00; PNFI = .62; PGFI = .52] but did not differ from the partially mediated model, $\chi^2_{difference}(1)$ = 1.17, ns. Given that the partially mediated model and nonmediated model provide equivalent fits to the data, the nonmediated model is accepted based on the consideration of parsimony.

Post hoc inspection of the model parameters suggested that the nonsignificant path from accident history to willingness to participate could be deleted from the model. Doing so did not change the fit of the model [$\chi^2_{difference}(1)$ = 1.70, ns; $\chi^2(31)$ = 33.77, ns; GFI = .95; AGFI = .90; RMSEA = .03; NFI = .93; CFI = .99; PNFI = .64; PGFI = .53]

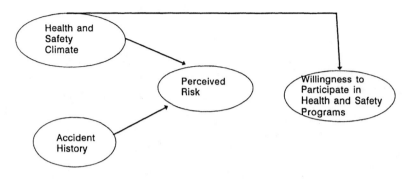

Figure 7.6.

but it did result in a more parsimonious model. The revised nonmediated model is presented in Figure 7.6.

Sample Results Section

A sample results section reflecting these findings is presented below.

Results

Descriptive statistics and intercorrelations for all study variables are presented in Table 7.12. All model tests were based on the covariance matrix and used maximum likelihood estimation as implemented in LISREL VIII (Jöreskog & Sörbom, 1992).

The measurement model provided an acceptable fit to the data [$\chi^2(29)$ = 30.89, ns; GFI = .95; AGFI = .90; RMSEA = .02; NFI = .94; CFI = 1.00; PNFI = .60; PGFI = .50]. Standardized parameter estimates for the measurement model are presented in Table 7.13.

Table 7.14 presents the fit indices for the three structural models of interest. As shown, the partially mediated model provided a better fit to the data than did the fully mediated model [$\chi^2_{\text{difference}}(2)$ = 8.72, p < .02]. The nonmediated model and partially mediated model did not differ [$\chi^2_{\text{difference}}(1)$ = 1.17, ns]. Based on the consideration of parsimonious fit, the nonmediated model was retained for further analysis.

TABLE 7.12 Descriptive Statistics and Correlations for All Study Variables ($N = 115$)

Variable	1	2	3	4	5	6	7	8	9	10
1. Participation 1										
2. Participation 2	76									
3. Participation 3	78	68								
4. Risk to self	-05	01	-05							
5. Risk to others	10	09	08	52						
6. Manager's commitment	01	08	14	-28	-22					
7. Supervisor's commitment	20	18	29	-44	-29	54				
8. Coworkers' commitment	22	25	29	-42	-31	57	65			
9. Accident history	00	00	-05	42	22	-13	-26	-20		
10. Witnessed accidents	12	03	11	26	30	-12	-20	-17	47	
Mean	10.7	8.9	10.9	18.6	3.8	5.5	5.7	5.5	1.7	0.9
SD	2.7	3.1	2.9	7.3	1.5	1.4	1.2	1.2	1.7	0.8

TABLE 7.13 Standardized Parameter Estimates for the Measurement Model

	Willingness to Participate	Risk	Health and Safety Climate	Accident History	R^2
1. Participation 1	0.92				0.85
2. Participation 2	0.82				0.67
3. Participation 3	0.85				0.72
4. Risk to self		0.85			0.72
5. Risk to others		0.61			0.38
6. Manager's commitment			0.66		0.43
7. Supervisor's commitment			0.80		0.64
8. Coworkers' commitment			0.83		0.68
9. Accident history				0.78	0.61
10. Witnessed accidents				0.60	0.36

TABLE 7.14 Fit Indices for the Three Models

	χ^2	df	GFI	AGFI	RMSEA	NFI	CFI	PNFI	PGFI
1. Partially mediated	30.9	29	.95	.90	.02	.94	1.00	.60	.50
2. Fully mediated	39.6	31	.94	.89	.05	.92	.98	.63	.53
3. Nonmediated	32.1	30	.95	.90	.03	.93	1.0	.62	.52

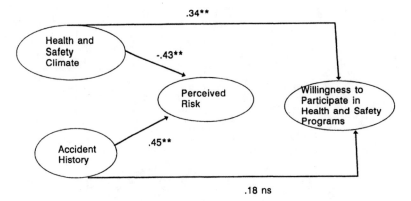

Figure 7.7.

Standardized parameter estimates for the structural model are presented in Figure 7.7. As shown, both risk perceptions ($\beta = -.43$, $p < .01$) and willingness to participate in health and safety programs ($\beta = .34$, $p < .01$) were predicted by perceived health and safety climate. Risk perceptions ($\beta = .45$; $p < .01$) but not willingness to participate ($\beta = .18$, ns) were predicted by respondents' accident history.

Deleting the nonsignificant path from the model did not result in a significant change to model fit, $[\chi^2_{difference}(1) = 1.70$, ns].

CHAPTER 8

Concluding
Comments

I n previous chapters, we considered the logic and mechanics of structural
equation modeling with specific reference to the three most common
versions of structural equation models: confirmatory factor analysis,
observed variable path analysis, and latent variable path analysis. In this
final chapter, I introduce two useful extensions to the procedures
discussed thus far.

Single Indicator Latent Variables

As a general rule, one should strive for at least two or three indicators
(observed variables) for every latent variable. Following this guideline
generally will steer you clear of the shoals of underidentified models. In
some cases, this rule must be violated because of either lack of available
data or lack of forethought.

Unfortunately, we are sometimes stuck with only one indicator for a
construct. Two solutions to this dilemma are possible. First, one can divide
the scale items to form multiple indicators, as was done in the previous
chapter. The second solution is to declare a latent variable with only one
indicator. This is bound to leave us with an identification problem
(trying to estimate both a unique and a common factor loading as well
as the variance for one construct using only one indicator). The solution
is to FIx the common (LY) and unique (TE) factor loadings at predetermined values and to estimate only the variance of the latent variable.

Specifically, we fixed the common factor loading (in the **LY** matrix) to be equal to the product of the reliability (alpha) and the standard deviation. If you understand reliability to measure the proportion of true score variance in a scale, this procedure essentially says X% of the variance in the observed score is true score variance. The unique factor loading (the diagonal element in the **TE** matrix) was fixed at a value equal to 1 – reliability × variance of the observed score. Again, this is simply an estimate of the percentage of error variance, which is all that is represented by the unique factor loading.

The one remaining case is when your single indicator is not a scale and you do not have any estimate of reliability for the variable. Fixing the factor loadings usually provides a workable solution to this problem. In this case, you only have to fix the common factor loading to equal 1 and the unique factor loading to equal 0 (assuming perfect reliability in the single item) to duplicate the procedure described above.

Simplifying Complex Models

If you recall the example of latent variable path analysis given above, you will remember that the LISREL code is rather complex. In formulating a model this way, you must keep track of the forms of all eight LISREL matrices at the same time. Moreover, you must keep track of the status (fixed, free) of every element in those matrices.

There is a way to reduce the cognitive complexity of latent variable models. Essentially, the procedure is to ignore the X-variable side of the LISREL model and to use only the Y side. As an illustration, below are two alternate model statements. Both describe exactly the same model and are mathematically equivalent (more important, they result in the same output).

```
MO NX = 7 NK = 3 NY = 5 NE = 2 PH = ST PS = DI,FR BE = FU,FI
   GA = FU,FI
MO NY = 12 NE = 5 PS = SY,FI BE = FU,FI TE = SY,FI
```

Note that both model statements reference 12 observed variables and five latent variables. The major differences are that I have eliminated all reference to the X variable matrices (**LX, PH, TD**) in the second statement, reducing my model to only four matrices (**LY, BE, TE,** and

PS). Also note that I have changed the specification of the **PS** matrix to be symmetrical and fixed rather than diagonal and free. This will allow me to estimate the correlations between the three exogenous variables (previously represented in the **PH** matrix). Thus, the **PS** matrix will now look like this:

	Eta1	Eta2	Eta3	Eta4	Eta5
Eta1	Free				
Eta2	Fixed	Free			
Eta3	Fixed	Fixed	Free		
Eta4	Fixed	Fixed	Free	Free	
Eta5	Fixed	Fixed	Free	Free	Free

The lines of code that would follow the second model statement would free the diagonal elements for all latent variables (variances) and free the covariances between the last three latent variables (which are the exogenous variables). The code is as follows.

```
FR PS(1,1) PS(2,2) PS(3,3) PS(4,4) PS(5,5)
FR PS(5,4) PS(5,3) PS(4,3)
```

The only difference this modification seems to make in the actual analyses (aside from the reduced demands on short-term memory) is that LISREL will report R^2 values for the exogenous variables, and these values will always be zero. This is because you do not predict any of the variance in three of the latent variables. Despite this minor difference, fit indices and parameter estimates will be exactly the same either way you set up the model.

Final Comments

Despite my somewhat tongue-in-cheek attitude, I have developed a great deal of respect for the power of LISREL to address increasingly complex research questions. In the foregoing, I have tried to illustrate some of the main types of questions that can be asked and answered using LISREL.

It is important to note that I have focused on the mechanics rather than the mathematical derivation or logical rigor of LISREL analyses.

Although this approach suited my goals in writing a researcher's guide, please be aware that I have glossed over many of the fine points of using LISREL. I leave you with the task of exploring these issues in more depth and the suggestion that the reference list following this chapter provides a good starting point for this exploration.

References

Akaike, H. (1987). Factor analysis and the AIC. *Psychometrika, 52,* 317-332.

Anderson, J. C., & Gerbing, D. W. (1984). The effect of sampling error on convergence, improper solutions, and goodness-of-fit indices for maximum likelihood confirmatory factor analysis. *Psychometrika, 49,* 155-173.

Anderson, J. C., & Gerbing, D. W. (1988). Structural equation modelling in practice: A review and recommended two-step approach. *Psychological Bulletin, 103,* 411-423.

Barling, J., Kelloway, E. K., & Bremermann, E. H. (1991). Pre-employment predictors of union attitudes: The role of family socialization and work beliefs. *Journal of Applied Psychology, 76,* 725-731.

Baron, R. M., & Kenny, D. A. (1986). The moderator-mediator variable distinction in social psychological research: Conceptual, strategic and statistical considerations. *Journal of Personality and Social Psychology, 51,* 1173-1182.

Bentler, P. M. (1980). Multivariate analysis with latent variables: Causal modelling. *Annual Review of Psychology, 1980, 31,* 419-456.

Bentler, P. M. (1985). *Theory and implementation of EQS: A structural equations program.* Los Angeles: BMDP Statistical Software.

Bentler, P. M. (1990). Comparative fit indexes in structural models. *Psychological Bulletin, 107,* 238-246.

Bentler, P. M., & Bonett, D. G. (1980). Significance tests and goodness of fit in the analysis of covariance structures. *Psychological Bulletin, 88,* 588-606.

Bentler, P. M., & Chou, C. P. (1987). Practical issues in structural equation modeling. *Sociological Methods & Research, 16,* 78-117.

Blalock, H. M. (1964). *Causal inference in non-experimental research.* Chapel Hill: University of North Carolina Press.

Bollen, K. A. (1989). *Structural equations with latent variables.* New York: John Wiley & Sons.

Bollen, K., & Lennox, R. (1991). Conventional wisdom on measurement: A structural equation perspective. *Psychological Bulletin, 110,* 305-314.

Bollen, K. A., & Long, J. S. (1993). Introduction. In K. A. Bollen & J. S. Long (Eds.), *Testing structural equation models.* Beverly Hills, CA: Sage.

Boomsma, A. (1983). *On the robustness of LISREL (maximum likelihood estimation) against small sample size and nonnormality.* Unpublished doctoral dissertation, University of Groningen, The Netherlands.

Bozdogan, H. (1987). Model selection and Akaike's Information Criterion (AIC). *Psychometrika, 52,* 345-370.

Brannick, M. T. (1995). Critical comments on applying covariance structure modeling. *Journal of Organizational Behavior, 16,* 201-213.

Breckler, S. J. (1990). Applications of covariance structure modeling in psychology: Cause for concern? *Psychological Bulletin, 107,* 260-273.

Browne, M. W. (1982). Covariance structures. In D. M. Hawkins (Ed.), *Topics in multivariate analysis* (pp. 72-141). Cambridge, UK: Cambridge University Press.

Browne, M. W., & Cudeck, R. (1989). Single sample cross-validation indices for covariance structures. *Multivariate Behavioral Research, 24,* 445-455.

Browne, M. W., & Cudeck, R. (1993). Alternative ways of assessing model fit. In K. A. Bollen & J. S. Long (Eds.), *Testing structural equation models.* Newbury Park, CA: Sage.

Cliff, N. (1983). Some cautions concerning the application of causal modeling methods. *Multivariate Behavioral Research, 18,* 115-116.

Cree, T., & Kelloway, E. K. (in press). Responses to occupational hazards: Exit and participation. *Journal of Occupational Health Psychology.*

Cudeck, R. (1989). Analysis of correlation matrices using covariance structure models. *Psychological Bulletin, 105,* 317-327.

Cudeck, R., & Browne, M. W. (1983). Cross-validation of covariance structures. *Multivariate Behavioral Research, 18,* 147-167.

Fishbein, M., & Ajzen, I. (1975). *Belief, attitude, intention and behavior: An introduction to theory and research.* Reading, MA: Addison-Wesley.

Friedman, L., & Harvey, R. J. (1986). Factors of union commitment: The case for lower dimensionality. *Journal of Applied Psychology, 71,* 371-376.

Fullagar, C. (1986). A factor analytic study on the validity of a union commitment scale. *Journal of Applied Psychology, 71,* 129-137.

Fullagar, C., McCoy, D., & Shull, C. (1992). The socialization of union loyalty. *Journal of Organizational Behavior, 13,* 13-26.

Gerbing, D. W., & Anderson, J. C. (1992). Monte Carlo evaluations of goodness of fit indices for structural equation models. *Sociological Methods & Research, 21,* 132-160.

Gordon, M. E., Philpot, J. W., Burt, R. E., Thompson, C. A., & Spiller, W. E. (1980). Commitment to the union: Development of a measure and an examination of its correlates. *Journal of Applied Psychology, 65,* 474-499.

Hayduk, L. A. (1987). *Structural equation modeling with LISREL.* Baltimore: Johns Hopkins University Press.

James, L. R., & James, L. A. (1989). Causal modeling in organizational research. In C. L. Cooper & I. Robertson (Eds.), *International review of industrial and organizational psychology, 1989* (pp. 371-404). Chichester, UK: John Wiley & Sons.

James, L. R., Mulaik, S. A., & Brett, J. M. (1982). *Causal analysis: Assumptions, models, and data.* Beverly Hills, CA: Sage.

Jöreskog, K. G. (1993). Testing structural equation models. In K. A. Bollen & J. S. Long (Eds.), *Testing structural equation models.* Newbury Park, CA: Sage.

Jöreskog, K. G., & Sörbom, D. (1992). *LISREL VIII: Analysis of linear structural relations.* Mooresville, IN: Scientific Software.

Kelloway, E. K. (1995). Structural equation modelling in perspective. *Journal of Organizational Behavior, 16,* 215-224.

Kelloway, E. K. (1996). Common practices in structural equation modeling. In C. L. Cooper & I. Robertson (Eds.), *International review of industrial and organizational psychology, 1996* (pp. 141-180). Chichester, UK: John Wiley and Sons.

Kelloway, E. K., & Barling, J. (1993). Members' participation in local union activities: Measurement, prediction and replication. *Journal of Applied Psychology, 78,* 262-279.

Kelloway, E. K., Catano, V. M., & Southwell, R. E. (1992). The construct validity of union commitment: Development and dimensionality of a shorter scale. *Journal of Occupational Psychology, 65,* 197-211.

Kenny, D. A., & Judd, C. M. (1984). Estimating the nonlinear and interactive effects of latent variables. *Psychological Bulletin, 96,* 201-210.

Klandermans, B. (1989). Union commitment: Replications and tests in the Dutch context. *Journal of Applied Psychology, 72,* 319-332.

Loehlin, J. C. (1987). *Latent variable models: An introduction to factor, path, and structural analysis.* Hillsdale, NJ: Lawrence Erlbaum.

Long, J. S. (1983a). *Confirmatory factor analysis: A preface to LISREL.* Beverly Hills, CA: Sage.

Long, J. S. (1983b). *Covariance structure models: An introduction to LISREL.* Beverly Hills, CA: Sage.

MacCallum, R. C. (1986). Specification searches in covariance structural modeling. *Psychological Bulletin, 100,* 107-120.

MacCallum, R. C., & Browne, M. W. (1993). The use of causal indicators in covariance structure models: Some practical issues. *Psychological Bulletin, 114,* 533-541.

MacCallum, R. C., Roznowski, M., & Necowitz, L. B. (1992). Model modifications in covariance structure analysis: The problem of capitalization on chance. *Psychological Bulletin, 111,* 490-504.

Marsh, H. W., Balla, J. R., & MacDonald, R. P. (1988). Goodness-of-fit indexes in confirmatory factor analysis: The effect of sample size. *Psychological Bulletin, 88,* 245-258.

McDonald, R. P., & Marsh, H. W. (1990). Choosing a multivariate model: Noncentrality and goodness of fit. *Psychological Bulletin, 107,* 247-255.

McGrath, J. E., Martin, J., & Kukla, R. A. (1982). *Judgment calls in research.* Beverly Hills, CA: Sage.

Medsker, G. J., Williams, L. J., & Holahan, P. J. (1994). A review of current practices for evaluating causal models in organizational behavior and human resources management research. *Journal of Management, 20,* 439-464.

Pedhazur, E. J. (1982). *Multiple regression in behavioral research: Explanation and prediction.* New York: Holt, Rinehart & Winston.

Raykov, T., Tomer, A., & Nesselroade, J. R. (1991). Reporting structural equation modeling results in *Psychology and Aging:* Some proposed guidelines. *Psychology and Aging, 6,* 499-503.

Schmitt, N. (1989). Editorial. *Journal of Applied Psychology, 74,* 884.

Steiger, J. H. (1990). Structural model evaluation and modification: An interval estimation approach. *Multivariate Behavioral Research, 25,* 173-180.

Stone-Romero, E., Weaver, A., & Glenar, J. (in press). Trends in research design and data analysis strategies in organizational research. *Journal of Management.*

Tabachnick, B. G., & Fidell, L. S. (1996). *Using multivariate statistics* (3rd ed.). New York: HarperCollins College Publishers.

Tanaka, J. S. (1993). Multifaceted conceptions of fit in structural equation models. In K. A. Bollen & J. S. Long (Eds.), *Testing structural equation models.* Newbury Park, CA: Sage.

Williams, L. J. (1995). Covariance structure modeling in organizational research: Problems with the method vs. applications of the method. *Journal of Organizational Behavior, 16,* 225-233.

Wright, S. (1934). The method of path coefficients. *Annals of Mathematical Statistics, 5,* 161-215.

Index

Absolute Fit, 23
  indices of, 24-29
Adjusted Goodness of Fit Index (AGFI),
  27
Akaike Information Criterion (AIC),
  32-33
Augmented moment matrix (AM), 47

Beta (BE) matrix, 44

Causality, 8,9
Chi-square, 24-26
  and degrees of freedom ratio, 28
  difference test, 36-37, 39
Coefficient of Determination. See R2
Comparative fit, 23, 29-32
Comparative Fit Index (CFI), 31
Condition 9 tests, 28-29
Condition 10 tests, 28
Confirmatory factor analysis, 2, 10
  example of, 54-80
  rival model specifications in, 33-35
Consistent Akaike Information Criterion
  (CAIC), 32-33
Correlation matrix (KM), 47, 48
Covariance matrix, 19
  CM, 47, 48

Cross-Validation Index, 31-32

Data (DA) keyword, 46
Discrepancy function, 26

Endogenous variables, 8
Equal (EQ), 51
Estimation, 7, 63-76, 87-101, 109-119,
  122-130
Exogenous variables, 8
Expected Value of the Cross Validation
  Index (ECVI), 32
Exploratory factor analysis, 2

Fitting criteria. See Model fit
Fixed elements, 42
  FI, 51
Free elements, 42
  FR, 51
Full information techniques, 18-19

Gamma (GA) matrix, 44
Generalized Least Squares, 18
Goodness of Fit Index (GFI), 27

Identification, 7, 14-16, 62-63, 86,
    108-109, 122
Incremental Fit Index (IFI), 31
Iterative estimation, 16

Just-identified models, 14

Labels:
    LA, 47
    LE, 51
    LK, 51
Lagrange multiplier test, 38
Lambda X (LX) matrix, 43
Lambda Y (LY)matrix, 44
Latent variables, 10
Latent variable models, 2
    example of, 102-134
LISREL:
    keywords, 41-54
    matrices, 41-45

Manifest variables. *See* Observed variables
Matrix (MA) keyword, 47
Matrix of moments (MM), 47, 48
Maximum Likelihood Estimation, 17-18
Means (ME), 49
Missing value (XM) keyword, 47
Model:
    command (MO), 49
    fit, 7, 8, 23-40, 76-78, 101, 119, 130
    fitting criteria, 17
    modification, 7, 20-22, 37-39, 101
    specification, 7-14, 55-62, 81-86,
        103-108, 119-122
Modification index, 38

NE, 43
Nested model comparisons, 33-37
NK, 43
Non-centrality parameter, 26, 31
Non-normed Fit Index (NNFI), 30-31
Non-recursive models, 15
Normed Fit Index (NFI), 30
Number of groups (NG), 46
Number of input variables (NI),46

Number of observations (NO), 46
NX, 43
NY, 43

Observed variables, 11
Optimal scores matrix (OM), 47, 48
Ordinary Least Squares, 18
Output (OU), 51-53
Over-identified models, 14

Parsimonious fit, 23, 32
    indices of, 32-33
Parsimonious Goodness of Fit Index
    (PGFI), 32
Parsimonious Normed Fit Index (PNFI),
    32
Path analysis, 2
    example of, 81-102
    rival model specifications in, 35-37
Path diagrams, 9-14
    rules for decomposing, 12
Phi (PH) matrix, 43
Polyserial correlations (PM), 47, 48
Psi (PS) matrix, 44

Raw Data (RA), 48
R2, 28
Recursive models, 15
Relative Fit Index (RFI), 31
Respecification. *See* Model modification
Results:
    guidelines for reporting, 78
    confirmatory factor analysis, 79-80
    latent variable models, 131-134
    observed variable path analysis,
        101-102
Root Mean Squared Error of
    Approximation (RMSEA), 27
Root Mean Squared Residual (RMR),
    27

Sample size, 20
Select (SE), 49
Simplifying complex models, 136-137
SIMPLIS, 42

Single indicator latent variables, 135-136
Specification search. *See* Model
    modification
Standard deviation (SD), 49
Strategy for assessing model fit, 39-40
Structural equation modeling, 1
    model of 7

t-rule for model identification, 14
Theta-Delta (TD) matrix, 43
Theta-Epsilon (TE) matrix, 44
Theory, 5

building, 38
    of reasoned action, 5, 18
    trimming, 20-21, 38
Two-stage modeling, 106-107

Under-identified models, 15

Value (VA), 51

Wastebasket parameters, 21

About the Author

E. Kevin Kelloway received his PhD in Organizational Psychology from Queen's University (Kingston, Ontario, Canada) in 1991 and is currently with the University of Guelph, where he holds the position of Professor in the Psychology Department. His teaching responsibilities include both undergraduate and graduate courses in Organizational Psychology, Statistics, Measurement, and Research Design. He is an active researcher, having published more than 40 articles and book chapters. His research interests include unionization, job stress, leadership, and the development of work attitudes/values. He is coauthor of *The Union and Its Members: A Psychological Approach* (1992) and *Flexible Work Arrangements: Managing the Work-Family Boundary* (forthcoming), as well as coeditor of *Youth and Employment* (forthcoming). With Julian Barling (Queen's University), he edits a book series titled *Advanced Topics in Organizational Psychology* (Sage Publications). He has published extensively using structural equation modeling techniques and authored a review of such techniques for the 1996 *International Review of Industrial/Organizational Psychology*.